Whisper to the Black Candle

Whisper to the Black Candle

Voodoo, Murder, and the Case of Anjette Lyles

by

Jaclyn Weldon White

MERCER UNIVERSITY PRESS

1979   1999

TWENTY YEARS OF PUBLISHING EXCELLENCE

ISBN 0-86554-638-X
MUP/ H476

First Edition.

Ant Terro ant poison is a registered trademark of the Senoret Chemical Company, Incorporated.

Velva Glo embalming fluid is a registered trademark of the Hydrol Chemical Company, Incorporated.

Champion Specialist embalming fluid is a registered trademark of the Champion Chemical Company, Incorporated.

Coca-Cola is a registered trademark of the Coca-Cola Company, Incorporated.

∞The paper used in this publication meets the minimum requirements of American National Standard for Information Sciences — Permanence of Paper for Printed Library Materials, ANSI Z39.48-1984.

Library of Congress Cataloging-in-Publication Data

White, Jaclyn Weldon.
Whisper to the black candle: voodoo, murder, and the case of Anjette Lyles / by Jaclyn Weldon White. — 1st ed.
p. cm.
Includes Index.
ISBN 0-86554-638-X
1. Murder — Georgia — Macon Case Studies. 2. Lyles, Anjette. 3. Voodooism — Georgia — Macon Case Studies. I. Title.
HV6534.M2W48   1999
364.15'23'09758552 — dc21   99-32054
                                             CIP

TABLE OF CONTENTS

ACKNOWLEDGMENTS

Special thanks to Charles Adams, Rosemary Reynolds and Byrice and Ollie Goings for their time and patience; to Nancy Dupree and Deborah Stone for their inspiration; to Harriet Comer for her guidance; to Carol Dossman for her assistance; to Margaret Anne Carswell and Suzy McCullough for their insight and hard work; to Bill Head for his expertise; to Carl, as always, for his constant support; and to my father, John Weldon, who started me on the path.

In researching this book, I was fortunate to have the use of the published accounts of the case in the *Macon Telegraph*, the *Atlanta Journal* and the *Atlanta Constitution*. I also made extensive use of the trial transcript, which numbered over 1,000 pages of text and exhibits. The city directories and old telephone books at the Washington Memorial Library provided a few of the exact locations I identified in the book.

Charles Adams, Byrice and Ollie Goings, Rosemary Reynolds and Celestine Sibley were all kind enough to meet with me and share their memories of the case and that time. I also spoke briefly by telephone with several of the jurors.

For Caroline Weldon Thompson, the brightest star in the heavens.

ILLUSTRATIONS

PRINCIPAL CHARACTERS

FAMILY:
Anjette Donovan Lyles — daughter, wife, mother, restauranteur, widow, defendant
Alice Donovan— Dole's wife and Anjette's sister-in-law
Jetta Donovan — Anjette Lyles's mother
William Donovan — Anjette Lyles's father
Ben F. Lyles, Jr. — first husband of Anjette Lyles
Marcia Lyles — Anjette Lyles's eldest daughter
Carla Lyles — Anjette Lyles's younger daughter
Julia Young Lyles — Ben Lyles's mother
Joe Neal Gabbert — Anjette Lyles's second husband

FRIENDS, ACQUAINTANCES AND EMPLOYEES:
Rosemary Reynolds — employee, friend and witness
Carrie Jackson — longtime cook at Lyles's Restaurant
Carmen Howard — Anjette Lyles's housekeeper
Jennie Ingle — nurse and confidante
Bob Franks — Anjette Lyles's last serious love interest

THE PROFESSIONALS:
Lester Chapman — Bibb County Coroner
L.H. Campbell — Bibb County Medical Examiner
James Wood — Bibb County Sheriff
William West — Bibb County Solicitor General
Oscar Long — Bibb County Superior Court Judge
Ollie Goings — Chief Jailer, Bibb County Jail
Byrice Goings — wife to Ollie, superviser of the jail kitchen, and friend to Anjette

THE ATTORNEYS:
Charles Adams — special prosecutor
William Buffington — lead defense attorney
Jack Gautier — defense attorney
H.T. O'Neal — special prosecutor
Roy Rhodenhiser — defense attorney

CHAPTER ONE

ANJETTE DONOVAN WAS A BEAUTIFUL BRIDE WITH SPARKLING eyes and a cloud of soft dark hair. She walked down the aisle of the Mulberry Street Methodist Church on her father's arm one bright October day in 1947, smiling so brightly the wedding guests couldn't help but mirror her happy expression. Ben Franklin Lyles, Jr., a local boy fresh out of the Army, waited nervously at the altar for his bride. Ten minutes later they walked back down the same aisle as husband and wife. They made a handsome couple.

Anjette came of age during the frightening and exciting years of World War II. She was the only daughter of William and Jetta Donovan who owned and operated a Macon, Georgia, produce company. The Donovan house on Lamar Street was a rambling, old, high-ceilinged place with a broad front porch and a tree-shaded yard. The Donovans had three children, but Anjette was William's favorite. He doted on the pretty, dark-haired child who charmed everyone she met.

Anjette and "Little Ben," as her new husband was called to distinguish him from his late father, set up housekeeping in the Biltmore Apartments on Poplar Street. There, on a hill overlooking the town, they could gaze down at night on the lights of Macon. They were only a couple of blocks from Donovan's Produce Company and within walking distance of Lyles's Restaurant, the family business Ben ran with his widowed mother and his younger brother Joe. Soon after his marriage, Ben bought out his brother's interest in the restaurant. Business was booming and the young couple's future was bright. America had won the war and anything and everything was possible now.

During the early days of her marriage, Anjette spent her time doing those things young brides did. She decorated their apartment, shopped, lunched with friends and kept house. But she was never too busy to stop by the restaurant. She was attracted to the bustle of the place and sometimes lent a hand in the kitchen or took food to the tables. The customers grew fond of this young woman who was always ready with a joke or a friendly word.

It was a surprise when Anjette became pregnant within weeks of the wedding, but she and Ben weren't unhappy about it. They wanted a family. This just meant they were starting earlier than they'd intended. Through the mild winter months that followed, they settled into the routine of married life and planned for the birth of their first child.

Warm weather returned as time for the birth neared. The summer of 1948 was a tense one. Internationally, Berlin was blockaded, food was being airlifted in and the world feared another war. At home, President Truman outraged southern politicians by proposing civil rights legislation. No one could turn on a radio without being barraged by doom and gloom.

A heat wave held Macon in a steamy grip. Anjette sometimes went downtown to one of the big movie houses to lose herself in a Hollywood production and luxuriate in the oasis of air conditioning, but she spent most of June and July sipping iced Coca-Colas in front of rotating fans in her apartment trying to stay cool while, on the radio, Peggy Lee sang about "Mañana" and Bing Crosby crooned "Now is the Hour." The days seemed a hundred hours long. Finally, on July 24, a Saturday when the temperature soared to the high nineties, Anjette gave birth to a daughter. She and Ben named the baby Marcia Elaine and, several days later, took her home to Poplar Street.

When Marcia was only six weeks old, Ben's mother Julia entered Macon Hospital for surgery and the entire operation of the restaurant fell to Ben. He put in long hours and many nights didn't come home until after his wife was asleep. One night he didn't come home at all. Anjette woke in the early morning hours to find his side of the bed empty. He was nowhere in the apartment. She telephoned the restaurant, but got no answer. As the minutes dragged by, her concern grew. She tried to fight the rising panic, reasoning that if he'd been hurt, someone would have called her. She wandered from room to room, unable to settle anywhere. Several times she slipped into the darkened nursery to check on the baby who was sleeping peacefully through this night.

Just before dawn, there was a knock at the door. Scared of what news might be waiting on the other side, Anjette opened it to find her mother standing there, holding the arm of an intoxicated Ben Lyles. He was unsteady on his feet and well beyond coherent speech, but docile enough to allow them to steer him into the bedroom where he collapsed across the bed.

Jetta Donovan was not a warm woman. She had always been quick to anger and that morning she was as furious as Anjette ever remembered. She told her daughter that someone who lived in one of the front apartments had called and woke her.

"They said Little Ben was sitting in front of the Catholic church there in an automobile, didn't know if he was dead or if he was drunk!" she told Anjette. "I came right to town and there he was."

It had taken Jetta several minutes to rouse Ben and get him into the apartment. Climbing the stairs with him had been nothing less than an ordeal. She described every step in angry detail and her tone of voice made it clear that Anjette should have somehow prevented this.

Ordinarily, Anjette would have tried to appease her mother, but Jetta's anger was a small problem compared to the major dilemma she now faced. The restaurant was due to open in less than two hours. Lyles's was an institution in Macon. Located in the downtown business district, they served three meals a day. Businessmen met there for breakfast. Lawyers discussed cases over lunch. Ladies took breaks from their shopping to indulge in pie and coffee. In the evenings, families came for dinner.

Anjette knew the place had to open, but Julia was still in the hospital and Ben was clearly in no shape to help. There was only one thing to do. She dressed hurriedly. Then she woke Marcia and dressed and fed her. She bundled the baby up against the early morning chill and, over her mother's objections, went into town. A little scared and unsure of herself, she managed to open the restaurant and conduct business more or less as usual that day.

As fall slipped into winter, Anjette spent more time at the restaurant than her husband did. Even after Julia Lyles returned to work, Ben stayed away from the business for days at a time.

"He quit working," Anjette said later. "Mrs. Lyles tried to get Ben to work, but he wouldn't. Instead he drank whiskey and gambled."

One night Ben wrecked the couple's car. Though he was unhurt, the car was damaged so badly it couldn't be driven. With no money to repair it or buy a new one, Anjette was suddenly dependent on family members for shopping, visiting, and traveling to and from work. At 5:00 A.M. every morning, Julia drove to Poplar Street where she picked up Anjette and Marcia and drove them to the restaurant.

While her mother and grandmother operated the business, the baby slept in a makeshift cradle in the restaurant's kitchen. When Marcia fussed or needed feeding or changing, it was just as often one of the restaurant staff as her own mother who tended to the child. She became everyone's baby, as accustomed to the kitchen sights, sounds and smells as another child might be to the surroundings of her nursery.

Anjette confided to friends that Ben was drinking up to three fifths of liquor a day and he expected her to keep him supplied. "When I come home at night, if he is out of whiskey," she complained, "I have to get out and walk back to town and buy it for him."

Although finances were strained and life with Ben was less than idyllic, Anjette wasn't unhappy. She had discovered she had a flair for business and, while Julia was always present, more and more of the decision making was left to her daughter-in-law. Running a busy restaurant and associating with a variety of people was exciting. She especially enjoyed dealing with the public and was never too busy for a friendly word or a quick hug. She soon began thinking of the restaurant as hers.

Ben's health was deteriorating. He had contracted rheumatic fever in the service and now his associated heart condition was worsening. His legs and feet swelled painfully. Finally he became ill enough that he was admitted to the Veterans Hospital in nearby Dublin where he was treated for symptoms associated with rheumatic fever. While a patient there, he was declared totally disabled. He applied for and received a government pension that provided disability payments of several hundred dollars a month.

Ben was released from the hospital a few days later and returned home, but he was still a sick man. "The doctors told him that if he kept drinking, it would kill him," Anjette told Jetta.

For a while, his health improved. Still unable to work, he spent most of his days resting, but the prognosis for a full recovery was good and the future looked brighter than it had for many months.

Anjette became pregnant again in the late summer of 1950, but unlike her first, this pregnancy was not an easy one. She gained more weight than she had with Marcia and developed phlebitis a month or so before her second daughter Carla was born on May 18, 1951. Her illness kept her out of work for several months and the daily running of the restaurant was left to Julia Lyles. A kind woman who was loved by the staff, Julia did her best, but she lacked her daughter-in-law's deft touch with people and business slacked off a bit. Ben was still not working, but that didn't prevent him from complaining frequently about his mother's management of the restaurant.

One day in June, without telling his wife or his mother, Ben sold the restaurant his family had owned for nearly thirty years to a local woman named Lola Meeks. She paid him $2,500 for it. Anjette was outraged. "How could you do that?" she demanded. "You never even mentioned it to me!" Ben didn't bother giving her an explanation. The restaurant had been his to sell and he had done so.

Anjette believed the restaurant was worth far more than he'd gotten for it. During her time there, she had increased both the clientele and the profits. There was no excuse for what Ben had done. The proceeds from the sale were quickly swallowed up to pay debts and, after a month or two, the family's only income was Ben's disability pension. Anjette told friends he was drinking again.

In frustration, she took the children and moved in with her brother Dole and his wife, Alice. The excuse she gave friends was that the move was necessary because of her health. The Donovans had a maid who could look after Marcia and Carla and help Anjette while she recovered from her illness. It wasn't until the fall of the year that they returned to Ben and the Poplar Street apartment.

Anjette hoped for a fresh start with her husband, but life with Ben was no better than it had been before she left. His health was still poor and their financial situation took a definite turn for the worse when the Veterans Department notified them in late 1951 that Ben's disability status was being upgraded from 100% to 10%. His monthly pension payment was reduced to $190. Anjette was forced to go to her relatives time and again for money and hand-me-down clothes for the children. It was a bitter experience for a proud woman.

In December, Ben developed a new and frightening symptom. At any hour of the day, blood would begin flowing from his nose, sending the house into turmoil—Ben shouting in alarm and Anjette rushing around for towels and ice packs. His doctors believed the nosebleeds were a complication of his heart problems and continued to treat him for that. But his condition grew worse instead of better. On January 23, 1952, he was admitted to Macon Hospital, moaning in pain and bleeding from the mouth and nose. Once they had settled him in a room and managed to stop the bleeding, the doctors began searching for the cause of the diverse symptoms he exhibited. His arms and legs were swollen, and from time to time, his whole body went rigid. He vomited frequently and suffered occasional bouts of delirium. At times his limbs twitched uncontrollably. The doctors ran test after test, but reached no conclusions.

Anjette and Julia kept demanding an explanation for his illness. Were these symptoms of rheumatic fever? Was there something they weren't being told? The doctors remained uncertain. Though several possibilities were suggested, they couldn't say for sure what was wrong with Ben Lyles. He lapsed into a coma soon after he was admitted. For two days, his wife and mother sat helplessly by his bedside until, on January 25, he died. After some discussion, the doctors finally decided the cause of death must have been encephalitis.

The Memorial Chapel on Cherry Street handled Ben's funeral. From there, the procession made its way to Cochran, a small town about forty miles southeast of Macon. Anjette, Julia and the children rode in a big, black car directly behind the hearse, winding along narrow country roads lined with trees that were bare and stark against a gray sky. Little Ben was laid to rest beside his father in the churchyard of the Antioch Baptist Church. Julia Lyles was inconsolable, but Anjette held herself stiff and didn't cry. She was now the sole support of the infant in her arms and the toddler fidgeting beside her at the graveside.

At twenty-six years old, Anjette Lyles was a widow with no marketable skills and no resources. Ben had left only a small insurance policy and much of that had gone toward funeral expenses. The restaurant was gone and there were no savings. Anjette continued to receive Ben's disability benefits, but they dropped to $150 a month at his death. Once again, she turned to her family.

"I didn't have money to buy milk for my children," she said years later. "My brother and his wife gave me a hundred dollars and they bought me a case of Pet Milk to fix formula with. My mother bought my clothes and Mother and Mrs. Lyles both clothed the children."

Keeping the apartment was out of the question, so she and the girls moved in with her parents. But it wasn't to the spacious old house of her childhood she returned. Anjette's father had recently turned over the operation of the produce company to his son Dole and gone to work as a conductor with the Central of Georgia Railroad. With their three children grown and gone, Jetta and William Donovan had moved from the old Victorian house on Lamar Street to a new one-story brick bungalow on Vineville Avenue. They needed less space and relished the prospect of living in a new house rather than one nearly as old as the century. They never planned on more than two people living there, but Anjette had nowhere else to go. She and the children crowded into the Donovan house and she began to rebuild her life.

Ben's mother kept in close touch with the relocated family. With Little Ben gone and her younger son Joseph stationed in the Navy on the other side of the country, she turned more and more to Anjette and her granddaughters for comfort. At first she was just a frequent visitor to the Donovan house, but as the months passed, she began staying with them for days at a time rather than face the emptiness of her own small house across town. In such close quarters, tempers flared occasionally, but, for the most part, the arrangement worked well enough. Marcia and Carla were the ones who benefited most from this situation. They always had a grandparent nearby to care for them. There were plenty of people to read them stories or take them for walks. William Donovan especially enjoyed the arrangement. Having four-year-old Marcia in the house was almost like returning to the days when his own daughter was a tiny child who climbed into his lap for a hug.

Anjette was a woman who knew what she wanted. She'd experienced running a business only to have it snatched away from her and she was determined to have that again. Less than three months after Ben's death, she found a job as bookkeeper at the Bell House Restaurant, working for Mr. and Mrs. J. B. Bryan. Eeager to please and always willing to go a bit beyond her normal duties, she made herself a popular employee. The driving force in her life was to learn every aspect of the restaurant business. She worked hard, saving every penny she could. No money was wasted on new clothes or other such luxuries, but, surprisingly, her looks didn't suffer. In fact, she was more attractive than she'd ever been. She'd lost the weight gained during her pregnancy and the dark hair that had grown prematurely silver gave her a sophisticated, almost glamorous appearance.

Hard work paid off. By the spring of 1955, Anjette was ready to make her move and right the wrong done by Little Ben when he sold their business out from under her. She secured two bank loans totaling $12,000 and bought back Lola's Restaurant. On April 4, it reopened as Anjette's.

The day she opened her restaurant, she had only one hundred dollars in the cash register. She had convinced George Barnett at the Mulberry Market to let her charge the first week's groceries, and had reached a similar arrangement with the Swift Meat Company. That spring morning she stood behind the cash register and surveyed the booths and tables, clean and set and ready for the first customers of the day. She was finally back where she knew she belonged.

The food at Anjette's was standard Southern fare—well-cooked vegetables, fried meat and freshly made biscuits and cornbread. The menu had changed little since Ben Lyles, Sr., opened the place in the 1920s. But it wasn't the food that brought customers back again and again. It was the charismatic personality of the owner.

The restaurant had always been a natural gathering place for anyone doing business in Macon and Anjette's presence now made it the place to see and be seen. Just dropping in for coffee was fun. Some of her regular customers took to referring to their informal gatherings there as the One O'clock Luncheon Club. The group became so well established that, when one of their number was out of town, he would send a postcard addressed to the club at Anjette's Restaurant. The postcards were always delivered to the right table.

Charles Adams, a young lawyer just starting out in private practice, was a frequent customer. "Going to her restaurant, you didn't think about the food as much as you thought about just being welcome," he remembered years later. "She hugged everybody's neck when they walked in the door. She would come to each table and sit down and talk. She had a personality that was terrific. It was a pleasure to go in her restaurant. In between meals, she'd walk out on the sidewalk and say, 'Hello, how you getting along?' or 'You coming to lunch with me?' You couldn't help but like her."

CHAPTER TWO

ANJETTE BOUGHT A RESTAURANT WITH A READY-MADE STAFF. Some had been with the establishment through several owners, beginning with Ben Lyles, Sr., and continuing through the years Lola Meeks had owned the place. There were three cooks—all black—and several waitresses—all white. In 1955 Georgia, the world was strictly segregated. Blacks used the back doors, attended inferior schools and drank only from designated water fountains. The races were even separated in the newspaper where each had its own society pages— reporting engagements, wedding announcements, club and church news—and its own obituaries. This state of affairs was no different at Anjette's Restaurant. There were separate restrooms for white and black employees and, though they were responsible for the preparation of all the food on the menu, the cooks would never have been seated or served in the front of the establishment. But even in this stringently regulated society, the boundaries between the races could blur. Social restrictions couldn't keep people from liking each other.

Rosemary Reynolds was just a few years younger than Anjette. A cook at the restaurant, she lived in a small frame house on the far side of the river and often walked the three or four miles to and from work. Fourteen-hour work days were the rule rather than the exception. Following the usual course of things, she and Anjette would have remained employer and employee with the wide gulf of segregation separating them, but there was a natural chemistry between the two that bridged the gap. They hit it off immediately. They shared a sense of humor and were comfortable in each other's company. Sometimes they gossiped and giggled in the kitchen like schoolgirls.

"Everybody loves her," Rosemary told her husband Arthur, describing her new employer. "She is a sweet person. She'd give you the shirt off her back."

Anjette was genuinely generous, giving presents to her employees for no particular reason and readily sharing what she had. The Monday after Easter, she arrived for work with a showy purple orchid pinned to her dress. Even though it was barely 6:00 A.M., food preparation was already underway. Bacon sizzled in skillets and pots of simmering grits steamed the air.

"I got this to wear to church yesterday," she explained. "Isn't it pretty?"

The other women in the kitchen admired it, but Rosemary was the most vocal.

"Why, Anjette, it's the prettiest thing I ever saw," she said. She moved closer to get a better look. "I never saw anything like that in my life."

Anjette put the big flower in the refrigerator to keep it from wilting during the workday and when the restaurant closed that night, she sent the orchid home with Rosemary. Rosemary learned to watch what she admired. Even a few casual words of praise could prompt Anjette to give her the object of her admiration. Rosemary didn't like feeling she was taking advantage of her employer.

Early in their association, Anjette decided that Rosemary shouldn't have to cook for her husband after working all day.

"Now Rosemary," she'd say as they were preparing to leave the restaurant, "fix a plate to take to Arthur. You don't want to cook tonight."

So most evenings, Rosemary and Arthur Reynolds dined on restaurant food in their house across the river.

Anjette couldn't stand to see anyone go hungry. When the down-and-out came asking for food, she routinely sent them to the alley back of the restaurant where the kitchen staff were instructed to feed them.

Anjette and Rosemary never socialized outside the restaurant. In that time, it would have been unheard of for the two women to go to a movie or have lunch together. But they did talk. They spent hours at the table in the kitchen, sharing confidences and the details of their lives, providing each of them with an insider's look at life in a nearly separate culture. Anjette had few close friends, and Rosemary probably knew more about her fears and feelings than anyone else in Macon.

As the friendship between the two women grew, so did the business. Most airline employees who flew into Macon spent their layovers at the Lanier Hotel, and Anjette's Restaurant was in easy walking distance. The pilots usually ate at least one meal there on every trip to Macon. One warm evening shortly after Anjette had taken over the restaurant's operation, Joe Neal "Buddy" Gabbert, Capitol Airways pilot and Air Force veteran, strolled down Mulberry Street to the restaurant with a co-worker. When the screen door closed behind him, he surveyed the busy place. Customers were coming and going and several waitresses rushed among the tables, but Anjette was the first person he really noticed. That was not unusual. It was rare that a man didn't notice the pretty, outgoing woman with the silver hair.

But Anjette had nothing on her mind but business that night. She was shorthanded and was trying to fill in out front as well as in the kitchen. She was arranging fried chicken on a plate when a waitress brought her an order for two steak dinners from Gabbert's table. She plopped two steaks on the griddle and dipped potatoes into the deep fryer. Fifteen minutes later, the same waitress carried the plates out to Gabbert and his colleague.

Buddy cut into his steak and immediately called her back. "This steak is overcooked. I ordered it medium rare."

The waitress apologized, took his plate back to the kitchen and told Anjette about the complaint. Anjette was too busy to do more than nod her head. She put another steak on the griddle where it sizzled until she judged it to be done the way the customer wanted. She arranged it on another plate, wiped her hands on a towel and took the plate into the dining room.

"Which one wanted the steak re-cooked?" she asked the waitress.

The woman indicated a big, handsome man in the front booth. Anjette put the plate in front of him and smiled her most winning smile.

"I'm so sorry that your steak wasn't cooked to suit you, sir. I'm Anjette Lyles. This is my restaurant. I hope this is better."

Buddy returned her smile and cut into the steak. "Thanks. It's just right."

"Enjoy your meal, sir."

He watched with admiration as she walked back into the kitchen.

By the time Buddy and his friend had finished their meal, Anjette was behind the cash register. He handed her his check and the money to cover it. When she gave him his change, their hands touched and the pilot grinned at her.

"Brown eyes," he said, "I'm gonna marry you."

His words didn't particularly impress her. Flirting customers weren't anything new, and she usually gave as good as she got. Buddy Gabbert was just another friendly diner.

Anjette had little interest in romance at that point in her life. While she enjoyed the attention her good looks brought her, most of her energy was invested in building her business. She wanted to be seen as a successful professional, despite a culture that often excluded women from such areas of achievement. The Elks Club in Macon was an example of such exclusion.

A place to see and be seen, the Elks Club was a popular gathering place for the professional elite of the town. New doctors and lawyers made sure they lunched there and many had their secretaries page them at the restaurant so that their names would be heard over the public address system. On weekend evenings, prominent Macon residents could be found there, eating, drinking, and dancing. But during the late weekday afternoon hours, it was the exclusive domain of the men of the town to meet for drinks and to wind down from the business day. Women didn't venture inside until dark, and then never without an escort.

Anjette could not accept these restrictions. The Elks Club was a place for business people and that's exactly what she was. She began stopping by one or two afternoons a week. She would have a drink and speak to people she knew, making the jokes she was famous for and sometimes visiting several tables before returning to her restaurant for the dinner rush. Her behavior made the men a bit uncomfortable, but they couldn't help enjoying her presence.

Like Anjette, Buddy Gabbert was not easy to dismiss. Every time he was in town, he headed straight for Anjette's, claiming his favorite booth and flirting outrageously with the owner. He pursued her enthusiastically, taking her out whenever she'd let him. When he was out of town, he called and wrote letters. Anjette blossomed in the glow of this determined young man's courtship. Gradually, she allowed herself to be distracted from business. He made her feel young, carefree and pretty—the way she had felt as a girl, before life began taking its heavy toll on her.

One night in June, Buddy told her he wouldn't be able to see her for a while. He explained he had decided to earn some extra money and was taking a month's leave of absence from Capitol Airways. He was returning home to Texas.

"A friend of mine owns a crop dusting business in Pecos and needs some help. And I can use the money. I've got some big plans." The way he said that let Anjette know those big plans included her.

After he left town, she missed him, but Buddy called frequently. When he invited her to join him for a few days in Texas, she jumped at the chance. .

She arranged for Julia to keep the children. She made up restaurant menus for several days in advance and gave the staff careful instructions for running the place in her absence. Rosemary Reynolds's silence spoke volumes about her disapproval of a single woman making such a trip, but Anjette didn't care. The next day she flew across the country to El Paso.

After a brief visit with his family, Buddy and Anjette drove to Pecos, where they stayed at the Lone Star Motel and Buddy eagerly showed Anjette around his native state. He introduced her to his friends and spent hours driving her around the countryside. In the evenings they went to honky tonks where they danced to "Hearts of Stone" and "Let Me Go, Lover." Anjette was an eastern girl who had never seen anything like the hot, flat west Texas landscape. She greeted every new sight with amazement.

"Just wait till you see Carlsbad Caverns," Buddy promised her.

They drove through the Guadalupe Mountains into New Mexico, arriving in Carlsbad late on the afternoon of June 24. After checking into a small motel, they found a restaurant and ordered dinner. During the meal, Buddy told her he wanted her to be his wife. This territory wasn't new. He'd proposed several times before without success. This time, however, Anjette agreed.

Buddy was like a kid on Christmas morning. He was so excited he could barely finish his meal. He wanted them to marry immediately. Anjette laughed at his eagerness, but willingly went along with his plans. Around 11:00 P.M., they found the police department and walked in.

"We want to get married tonight," Buddy announced.

The sleepy man at the desk tried to talk them out of it.

"Tonight? Look, there's nobody here who can do that tonight. There's a judge who could marry you first thing in the morning. He'll be at the courthouse by nine o'clock. Why don't you come back then?"

But Buddy was adamant. He'd finally gotten Anjette to agree to marriage and he wasn't taking any chance on her changing her mind. He kept after the man, asking about justices of the peace and people in nearby towns who might perform the ceremony. Eventually, the desk sergeant agreed to see what he could do. He called around, got a judge out of bed and persuaded him to come to the courthouse. Anjette and Buddy were married just before midnight. They never did get to visit the famous caverns.

When the newlyweds returned to Macon, Buddy moved in with Anjette, the children and the Donovans on Vineville Avenue. The house was bursting at the seams in the summer and fall of 1955. In addition to Anjette and Buddy and the two children, Mrs. Lyles still stayed there most nights and, for a while, Jetta Donovan's brother and sister lived there as well.

"The reason we're staying there instead of moving out," Anjette told a friend, "is because Buddy goes out on trips. He can be gone as much as a week at a time. There's no sense really in me moving out because I'd have to be by myself so much. And the children have lived there ever since they were just babies. My father really wants us to stay because he loves the children so much."

Anjette's business was doing well and Buddy continued to fly for Capitol Airways. It seemed the sky was the limit for the young couple. The future was sunny and they started talking about buying a house of their own. Then, in October, Buddy began having problems with his wrist. He had broken it a few years before and a pin had been inserted when it was set. He'd grown used to occasional twinges of pain, but now it seemed to hurt all the time. The doctor he consulted suggested that the pin might be pressing on a nerve and recommended minor surgery to remove it. On November third, Buddy entered Parkview Hospital for the procedure. The operation took less than an hour and was a success.

They planned to keep him only overnight, but the next day he had developed a severe skin irritation. It began with swelling in his face and rapidly progressed over the next few days to the point that his chest, arms and upper legs were covered with an itching, stinging, oozing rash. This was accompanied by acute swelling. His body retained so much fluid that the nurses eventually had to puncture his feet with needles to allow it to drain.

Anjette stayed with him much of the time, but could only watch and wait. His eyes were swollen almost shut, and even though narcotics were administered regularly, he was often in extreme pain.

"Just let me die," he whimpered to the nurses who came in to administer medication. "Let me die."

The doctors' first guess as to the cause of the rash was a reaction to the anesthesia he'd been given during the operation, but as time passed and his condition worsened, a dermatologist was called in. Dr. R.M. Reifler first saw Buddy five days after he was admitted. His skin looked as if it had been burned to the point of blistering, and Reifler suspected he'd had some contact with a strong irritant.

"Buddy," he asked, "have you ever been exposed to any kind of poison? Like arsenic?"

The man on the bed, his head swathed in bandages to keep him from scratching his face any more, managed to answer. "No, no."

"Now, think. Have you been around pesticides?"

"Crop dusting."

But that didn't sound likely to the doctor. The type of insecticides used by crop dusters didn't usually contain arsenic.

"Were you ever treated for syphilis?" Reifler asked. In the not too distant past, arsenic had been used to combat that disease.

"No!"

The doctor didn't pursue the matter any further. He ran a few tests, but never reached a firm diagnosis. So he began treating the symptoms rather than speculating further about the cause.

Anjette asked over and over if Buddy were going to recover. She seemed to believe something terrible was going to happen to him. Since it had been only four years ago that she'd stood beside another husband in another hospital bed and watched him die, her reaction wasn't difficult to understand. And, as had been the case during Little Ben's illness, the doctors couldn't seem to decide what was wrong.

One morning Anjette left Buddy's bedside and stepped into the hallway. Bessie Treace was passing by.

"Nurse, can you come in my husband's room?"

Bessie did as she was asked, and Anjette pulled back the bed sheet.

"Look at his legs and feet," she told the nurse. "See if they aren't turning dark."

Treace looked. Gabbert's legs did appear darker than the rest of his body and she told his wife so.

"He's going to die," Anjette said. "I know he's going to die."

The nurse didn't know how to respond to that. She murmured some vague words of reassurance and hurriedly returned to her work, leaving Anjette by the bed, staring down at her husband.

Trying to run the restaurant while spending most every night at the hospital was bringing Anjette to the edge of exhaustion. The doctors suggested she hire a private duty nurse to attend to Buddy during the night shift. Jennie Ingle came well recommended. She arrived for her first shift on the evening of November seventh.

Jennie was used to keeping her feelings to herself when she was with patients, but she couldn't suppress a sympathetic grimace the first time she saw Buddy Gabbert. His whole body was covered by a weeping rash that caused severe itching. In places he'd clawed his skin until he bled. But he was alert and, in spite of his condition, managed to talk with his new nurse.

"I'm doing okay." His voice was hoarse. "If I could just stop scratching. I'm afraid I'm not going to have any skin left."

Ingle shared his concern and suggested a radical measure. "Why don't we tie your hands to the bed rail so it will remind you not to scratch?"

Buddy thought it was worth a try. She tied his hands with a soft cord and he soon drifted into a restless sleep. When he woke the next morning, there was no fresh blood on the sheets.

The experiment was such a success that when she came on duty the next night, the first thing Buddy said was, "Come on, Ingle, tie me down so I can go to sleep."

Gabbert's condition gradually improved. On November 13, the doctors released him from the hospital. Anjette drove him back to her parents' house where the family greeted him with an impromptu welcome home party. The mood was light and everyone expected him to make a full recovery.

But his condition began to deteriorate almost immediately. His doctor stopped by several times to see him and prescribed additional medication. When that didn't bring the improvement he'd hoped for, he suggested a private nurse be hired to help the family care for him. Anjette called Jennie Ingle again.

On a cold, windy night in late November, Jennie drove out to Vineville Avenue. She'd been surprised to hear from Anjette again. Buddy had been relegated to that place in her memory with all her other former patients. He'd seemed well on the road to recovery the last time she'd seen him. But now two weeks later, she was knocking on the door of this small brick house ready to nurse him back to health a second time.

Anjette let her in, and with hardly a word led her down the hall to a small bedroom where Gabbert lay. Jennie didn't mean to gasp, but she couldn't help it. He was again covered with the rash. All exposed skin was red, raw and wet-looking. His eyes were nearly buried in swollen flesh, his lips enlarged and cracked, and his ears inflamed and scaly.

"Hi, Ingle," he croaked in a weak voice.

Jennie did what she could to make him comfortable, but the medication he was taking brought little relief. He was terribly weak and unable to keep anything in his stomach. After the first night, Jennie stopped offering him solid food because it produced such violent spasms of nausea, but she kept trying liquids. She and Anjette took turns holding glasses of juice, Coca-Cola and tea to his lips while he sipped them. Sometimes he was able to keep it down, but more often he vomited up everything he was given. Dehydration was becoming a problem. By telephone, Jennie got the doctor's permission to administer glucose intravenously. It wasn't an easy task.

"I can't get the needle into his arms where the rash is so bad," she told Anjette and Jetta. "I don't think I can get through the scars."

She finally managed to insert the IV needle into a vein in his foot.

But Buddy didn't improve. He now had periods of irrationality, thrashing about, raving, and crying, as the women struggled to keep him in bed. Anjette and her mother looked after him during the day while Jennie kept the vigil at night. Sometimes Anjette joined the nurse in the darkened sickroom and the two women talked in whispers while he slept his restless, drug-induced sleep a few feet away.

On the fourth day of her assignment, Jennie tried for several minutes, but could no longer find a vein for the IV. It was past midnight, but she found Anjette and her mother at the kitchen table, sipping coffee. The long days were wearing on Anjette. She looked haggard with limp hair and dark circles under her pretty eyes. Jennie took a chair across from them.

"I can't find a vein for the IV," she told Anjette. "If something isn't done immediately, your husband will die."

The situation was overwhelming. Anjette didn't know how to handle this, but she nodded. "I'll do what I can tomorrow to get him into the Veterans Hospital in Dublin."

Jennie went home when her shift ended. The sun was rising as she climbed into bed, still wondering if there were something more she could have done to help Buddy Gabbert. She'd slept only a few hours when she was awakened by a telephone call.

"Ingle, all the arrangements are made." Anjette sounded exhausted. "We're taking Buddy to Dublin this evening."

"That's good."

"Will you come with us? Will you ride in the ambulance with him?"

Jennie agreed.

It was already dark when Ingle arrived at the Donovan house. Her patient was lying on his bed, dressed and docile and ready to go.

"I gave him one of those sedatives," Anjette told her. "That should keep him quiet until we reach the hospital."

Buddy was anxious to leave.

"Where's the ambulance?" he asked. "Why are they late?"

Anjette reassured him it wouldn't be much longer. When the ambulance finally arrived and the attendants brought the stretcher into the house, the sick man moved slowly from his bed and climbed onto it, refusing any assistance.

"Let's go," he told them.

Ingle climbed into the back of the ambulance with him and tried to make him comfortable. But every move he made opened more sores on his body and he was in agonizing pain. Anjette followed in her car.

What should have been a routine transport by ambulance suddenly turned frantic. Delirious from the pain and the drugs, Buddy tried to get out of the moving vehicle. Shouting that he was going to ride in the car, he managed to get up and wrench the rear door open before a desperate Jennie Ingle forced him back down on the stretcher and held him there with the weight of her body. When they arrived at the hospital, she felt like she'd fought a battle. It was a relief to get out of the vehicle and walk through the emergency entrance. She was more than ready to turn her difficult patient over to other hands. But her announcement that she'd brought Gabbert to them was met with blank stares.

"Why on earth did you come at this time of night?" one of the staff asked irritably.

"Gabbert?" a second woman asked, flipping through some papers. "I don't show anything for Gabbert. Did you bring his records? Charts? What did his doctor say?"

Neither Jennie nor Anjette had any records.

"I don't understand," Anjette said. "I thought it was all arranged."

Jennie tried to reassure her. "It'll be all right. It's just a mix up. They'll take care of him."

Buddy was in dreadful shape and that fact wasn't lost on the staff in the admitting office. With the patient lying there still strapped to the stretcher and Jenny and Anjette standing by, they made several telephone calls, searching for someone to give them the authority to admit him. Finally about 10:00 P.M., they found a doctor who was willing to give his permission and Buddy was admitted and placed in the psychiatric ward.

"It's not so busy in that ward," the admitting nurse told Anjette. "He'll get more attention there."

It was after 1:00 A.M. when Jennie and Anjette left for Macon. Nine hours later, the two women returned to Dublin. They drove slowly through a steady rain and discussed the very real possibility that Buddy might not recover.

"Do you have life insurance on him?" Jennie asked. Her career had taught her to be practical.

Anjette nodded. "And his mother won't see a penny of it. I've seen to that."

Ingle wasn't surprised by the animosity in the other woman's voice. Anjette had made no secret of her dislike for her husband's family. That, too, was something Jennie had seen a lot of over the years.

She stayed with Anjette all that day and the next, trying to help her pass the long hours and sitting with her by Buddy's bedside when they were allowed. By the second day of December, it was clear to the doctors that Buddy would not recover. Early that evening his kidneys failed and soon afterwards his life slipped away.

The attending doctor found Anjette pacing the corridor outside her husband's room.

"Mrs. Gabbert," he said as gently as he could, "your husband has passed away."

Like a woman in a trance, she nodded. Her face was free of all expression. He took her arm and led her to a chair in the waiting room. Ingle trailed along behind them.

"I don't want to make this any worse for you, Mrs. Gabbert," the doctor continued, "but we'd like to have an autopsy performed on your husband."

"You mean cut him up?"

"It's very important. We did everything humanly possible to save him. Everyone worked so hard. We really want to find out what killed him."

As the doctor droned on in his calm, professional voice, Anjette's control broke. She burst into tears. "No," she wailed. "I promised him I'd never let anyone cut him up."

She sobbed and whimpered, becoming more and more upset as the doctor tried to explain the need for the procedure. Exasperated, he finally told her he didn't have to have her consent and left her crying in the waiting room.

After a bit, the tears subsided. She took a few shuddering breaths and dried her eyes. There would be no more public shows of grief.

Ingle spent much of the next several days with her. As she planned her husband's funeral, Anjette worried that Buddy's family would try to interfere. "I know his mother will want to take him back, but the law's on my side. A widow can keep the body where she wants it."

As she predicted, the Gabberts did want their son's body shipped home to Texas, but Anjette refused to allow it. Instead his family flew to Macon for the funeral, and in the late afternoon of December 4, services for Buddy were held at Memorial Chapel. Anjette moved through the day like a robot, answering when spoken to but showing no emotion. She sat unmoving as she listened to the minister saying farewell to Buddy in the same chapel where, on a winter day four years before, she'd heard the same words spoken over Ben.

Heavy fog made for a slow, dreary drive to historic Riverside Cemetery where Buddy Gabbert was laid to rest.

CHAPTER THREE

"TEACH ME TO MAKE AN OMELETTE, ROSEMARY," MARCIA Lyles asked. "Please, please, teach me."

Rosemary Reynolds smiled down at her. Seven year old Marcia wasn't an especially pretty child, with her lank brown hair and slightly pudgy body, but she was sweet and eager to please and Rosemary enjoyed indulging her. "Okay, baby, I'll show you."

They'd done this before, so Marcia knew the routine. She dragged a wooden chair over to the counter and climbed up so she was standing beside the cook.

"Now be careful. That stove is hot."

"I will."

Rosemary cracked three eggs into a bowl, then solemnly placed it in front of Marcia and handed her a fork. Lower lip clamped between her teeth in concentration, the little girl beat the eggs, using the rotating motion she'd been shown. From across the room, her mother watched them, smiling. Life was finally returning to normal. With the past behind her and the arrival of a new year, she and her family could look to the future again.

Anjette had recovered quicker from Buddy's death than people expected. The reason became clear as the weeks passed and friends learned that her marriage hadn't been as happy as she'd pretended. She rarely spoke of him now, and when she did, it wasn't with love.

"You know," she confided to Jennie Ingle over lunch one day, "Buddy could be mean to me. He even raised his hand to me a few times."

"No!" Ingle said. "He *hit* you?"

Anjette shook her head. "No, but he tried sometimes. I don't know why I ever married him. I couldn't have stayed with him if he'd lived."

She sparked a flurry of gossip when, only a couple of months after Buddy's death, she began dating Bob Franks. He was a captain with Capitol Airways and had at one time been Gabbert's boss. After Buddy died, Franks started coming to the restaurant to check on the young widow. Some nights the two would sit and talk for hours. It was an easy progression from there to dating.

The sight of Anjette being squired around town by a handsome man only weeks after her husband's death raised quite a few eyebrows, especially since she seemed to be having such a good time. But Anjette wouldn't let it bother her. She wasn't going to pretend grief when she felt none. Macon would just have to talk.

As if to further remove herself from the past, Anjette retained a local attorney, J. Taylor Phillips, and had her name changed back to Lyles. She also decided to splurge a bit with Buddy's insurance money.

On a day in late February Anjette telephoned Lehman Myers, a used car dealer in Macon, with a specific request.

"I want a Cadillac. A white Cadillac."

"Now, Miz Lyles, are you sure it has to be white? I've got a nice blue one right here on the lot."

"No. I've got my heart set on white."

"Well, that shouldn't be too hard to locate. I'll call around and see what I can find."

Within twenty-four hours, Myers had located the Caldillac and called the restaurant. "I've found just what you want, Miz Lyles. A white Cadillac—a real beauty. It's in stock at Daniel's Chevrolet over in Swainsboro."

"Let's go get it!" she said eagerly.

That same afternoon, she drove her Oldsmobile the hundred or so miles to the little country town of Swainsboro. Lehman Myers and Bob Franks made the trip with her. The car she wanted was waiting at the dealership, freshly washed and gleaming in the pale winter sun. Anjette was not disappointed. She handed over the Oldsmobile keys on the spot and wrote a check for the difference. The Cadillac was hers.

Winter relinquished its hold on the South early that year. March was unusually mild, filled with sun, soft breezes and the pastel blooms of azaleas and dogwoods. Yellow jonquils appeared overnight in most front yards, and the primary colors of tulips glowed in the grassy medians on Mulberry Street. Anjette was a happy woman that spring.

Her children were thriving, her business was successful and she thought she just might be falling in love. Strolling along Mulberry Street one bright afternoon, she ran into Jennie Ingle.

"Oh, Jennie, I'm flying high!" she declared.

Jennie believed it. When she'd last seen Anjette in January, the poor woman was still haggard from the stress of Gabbert's illness and death. But today she was smiling, bubbling with energy and optimism.

"Come, go for a ride with me in my new car," she suggested.

As the big Cadillac glided through downtown traffic, the two women caught up on each other's lives. Anjette had missed Jennie. The nurse had been with her through some of the roughest times of her life and she felt she could confide in her. She took a deep breath and announced she was seeing someone new.

"Really?"

"Yes. His name is Bob Franks and he's wonderful! He's a pilot, like Buddy. In fact, he used to be Buddy's boss. He's flying in this afternoon." She gave a little laugh. "I'm going out to the airport in just a little while to pick him up. This is it, Ingle! I'm in love this time for sure."

Jennie hoped so. Anjette had known more heartache in her thirty or so years than most people saw in a lifetime. She deserved some happiness.

That summer Anjette decided she was ready to set up housekeeping on her own again. She and the girls moved out of the Donovans' place into a new split-level house in a quiet subdivision north of town. The house on Pinewood Drive had three bedrooms and two bathrooms. After the crowded conditions on Vineville Avenue, it seemed incredibly spacious. Anjette rented, and later bought, the house from Mrs. J. B. Bryan, her former employer. As soon as they were settled, Julia Lyles moved in with them. They hired Carmen Howard to keep house for them. Marcia started the third grade in September and Carla began kindergarten.

The Mulberry Street restaurant had been a part of the Lyles family for over thirty years and the tradition continued for Anjette's daughters. There were few days in their lives that did not include some time spent at the restaurant. Carmen looked after Carla during the day. When school was over, she picked up Marcia and then delivered both girls to their mother at the restaurant. Their usual playroom was the kitchen where the cooks and waitresses spoiled them with treats and privileges, but the children had free run of the place. Sometimes their natural exuberance got the best of them and they'd tear from the kitchen to the front sidewalk, whooping and hollering as they darted among the diners, until Anjette called them down. Their evening meals were usually eaten at the old table in the kitchen and it was rare that they went home before the establishment closed.

During the years after Ben's death, every penny had been carefully watched. Marcia and Carla were regularly dressed in hand-me-downs. Anjette had hated doing that, but there had been no alternative. Now, for the first time in years, there was a little extra money and she made a point of spending some of it on her children. She enjoyed dressing them in pretty clothes and being able to give them some of the dolls and toys they wanted. Once or twice a month, the three of them walked the few blocks to the Junior Bootery, a fashionable children's clothing store, where Anjette bought each girl a frilly new outfit.

Julia Lyles was a fixture in the restaurant. She came in early each day and often stayed until closing time, just as she had in the years she and Ben, Sr. ran the place. The continuity was comforting to her and being there filled some of the empty hours in her life. She wasn't paid a salary, but didn't seem to mind and cheerfully helped out whenever she was needed. If there was no work for her to do, she could be found in the kitchen, sewing or gossiping with the cooks. When Carla or Marcia needed a hug or a lap to cuddle in, Julia was always available with just the right amount of grandmotherly attention.

In all parts of the world, superstition has played a role in human belief and Macon was no exception. It wouldn't have been hard to find people there in 1956 who were uneasy with thirteen at dinner or preferred that black cats not cross their paths. But Anjette went far beyond that. She fervently believed in magic and was fascinated by all facets of the occult. William Hutchinson got a demonstration of her beliefs one summer evening when he came to pick up his wife, Cleo, after her waitressing shift ended.

He found her in the kitchen with Anjette, finishing up the end-of-the-day chores. On the table, protected by an upturned glass jar, a fat red candle was burning. Every now and then, the flame wavered and flared as if disturbed by a puff of wind. William couldn't understand how any stray breeze could find the candle behind its glass case. Anjette saw him staring and smiled knowingly.

"Bob Franks is coming in tonight. When it moves like that, it means he's getting closer."

Something about her tone of voice made him look closely at her face, but there was nothing there to suggest she was anything but serious.

On their way home, William asked Cleo about the candle.

"Oh, she has them burning all the time," she said. "All different sizes and colors. She talks to them, too."

Most of her friends and family knew about Anjette's peculiar beliefs. She used a variety of candles and was always willing to tell them more than they wanted to know about the purpose for each one. The tall green ones with the Lord's Prayer on them, called St. Anthony's candles, were supposed to burn for seven days without going out and brought luck or money. White candles were for peace and red for love. The orange candles were supposed to keep people from gossiping about you. Anjette burned them all from time to time, choosing the color most appropriate for the circumstances. Sometimes she put notes or photographs beneath the candle to accomplish a specific purpose.

Once a candle was lit, Anjette would whisper to it.

"Why you talking to that candle?" one of the cooks asked her one day.

"When you light it, you talk to it." She held a match to the wick of the orange candle, and with her other hand, sprinkled a bit of salt onto the flame. "You tell it what you want it to do. Just like you talk to all the other candles."

The cook just chuckled and shook her head, but Anjette didn't mind. She was secure in what she believed.

Carmen Howard was so accustomed to encountering voodoo paraphernalia in Anjette's house that she simply moved the assortment of candles, roots and powders from one spot to another when she cleaned. She wasn't a believer in such things herself and was more amused than disturbed by these discoveries. But there was one aspect of Anjette's preoccupation with the occult that Carmen didn't like one bit. Once a week or so, her employer had Carmen drive her to a ramshackle house near the cotton mill out in Vineville. There, while Carmen waited in the car, Anjette went inside and consulted with the old man who lived there. Carmen didn't like the area. Some rough people lived there and it was a dangerous place to be. And she didn't like sitting alone in the car as darkness fell while Anjette had her fortune told and spent more money on roots and candles.

In October, Julia Lyles was diagnosed with breast cancer and entered the hospital for a mastectomy. The older woman was frightened, but Anjette stayed with her most of the time, reassuring her that everything was going to be all right and bringing her little treats from the restaurant. When Julia was sent home a week later, the doctors assured her the surgery had been a success and she would completely recover. In a few weeks she would be able to resume her normal activities. By December, Julia was once again coming to the restaurant every day.

Her mother-in-law's bout with cancer had started Anjette thinking. She knew Julia had considerable savings and urged the older woman to make a will. "It's something everybody ought to do," she told her. "I'm going to get one myself."

"I don't want to talk about it," Julia said. "I've seen too many problems come up because of wills and I won't have one."

Anjette had heard the story before. Some years back, someone in the Lyles family had left a will that was contested and eventually broken. The episode caused such hard feelings that the division in the family had never been mended. But to Anjette, that wasn't a good enough reason not to do the responsible thing now. She decided to get some advice when she had the chance.

On a slow afternoon J. Taylor Phillips was passing the time drinking coffee in Anjette's when the proprietor joined him to ask his opinion of the problem of Julia and the will. She showed him two bankbooks in Julia's name from two Atlanta banks. Phillips was astonished by the totals—one was over $40,000 and the other near $50,000. He'd had no idea Julia Lyles was so well off and said so.

"I know," Anjette said impatiently, "but she won't be sensible about it. I've told her over and over to make a will, but she won't. I just don't know what to do."

Phillips knew there was no simple answer. If Julia didn't choose to make a will, no one could force her to do so. There were always problems when someone died intestate. He described what could happen and suggested that Anjette relay that information to her mother-in-law.

Bob Franks now flew into Macon regularly and often spent his layovers at the house on Pinewood Drive. He was such a frequent visitor that Anjette gave him his own key to the place. When his schedule took him elsewhere, she sometimes joined him, leaving Rosemary in charge of the restaurant. She tried to be discreet about these trips, inventing friends in distant towns and reasons to visit them, but no one was fooled by her stories.

"A lot of things she does," Rosemary told her husband, "she won't come to me with it. I know she's going to where he is, but she won't tell me that. She says she's going with friends. She doesn't want me to think bad of her. But I know."

Rosemary never confronted her. If Anjette wanted to pretend no one knew she was off with Franks, that's just what she would do.

Christmas that year was quite a contrast to the previous one. The Lyles family was in high spirits and Anjette was happiest of all. She enjoyed shopping and giving presents, and that year was able to do more than she had in the past. One December night she closed the restaurant early and threw a big party for the staff. She provided all the food and the drinks and gave each employee a gift.

But the good times stopped in February. William Donovan became ill. By the end of the month he was dead. Anjette was overcome with grief much deeper than any she'd felt for her husbands. She had adored her father and had always known she was his favorite. With William gone, her world was suddenly a colder, emptier place. The cheerful, outgoing Anjette disappeared, replaced by a woman who could barely manage a smile. She still went through her daily routine, seeing to her family and running the restaurant, but her lively spirit was missing. Sometimes she shared her pain with Rosemary and allowed herself to cry.

"You know," she said one day, "my mother has never told me she loves me. Daddy loved me, but Mother has never put her arms around me and told me she loves me."

The grief gradually subsided. As the months passed, she began taking an interest in things again, and by the time the warm weather returned, she was nearly back to her old self.

In June of 1957, Anjette suddenly gave in to the repeated requests from Buddy Gabbert's parents and agreed to have his body returned to Texas. Perhaps her own father's death had helped her understand their need to have their son nearby. Buddy was disinterred and flown to El Paso where the Gabberts held a memorial service for him. Before he was buried a second time, his mother slipped a small white Bible, opened to the book of John, inside the casket.

In August, Julia again became ill. She grew pale and listless and, even in the summer heat, was often chilled. Some days, just walking from the front of the restaurant to the kitchen taxed her to the limit of her strength. The staff was worried; even the customers grew concerned. Anjette repeatedly suggested she see a doctor.

"I don't want to. I don't want to find out what is wrong. Maybe it will just go away."

It wasn't an unusual attitude for a woman who'd already battled cancer once, but one August afternoon, her condition became too serious to ignore. Anjette had left the restaurant around 3:30 P.M., as was her habit, intending to rest for a while, then return for the dinner rush. Julia had stayed behind. About 4:00 P.M., she became violently ill. Cleo Hutchinson made a frantic call to Anjette.

"You'd better come get Mrs. Lyles," she said. "She's real sick, vomiting blood and turning purple! She needs to see a doctor."

Anjette sighed. "I can't do anything with her, Cleo." She was exhausted. Up since daybreak, she'd just gotten home and taken off her work clothes. She didn't relish the thought of driving back to the restaurant and having the same old argument with Julia about seeing a doctor. "I'll send Carmen to get her."

When the maid brought the older woman home, there could be no doubt she was very sick. Anjette helped her undress and get into bed.

"You going to call the doctor?" Carmen asked when Anjette returned to the kitchen.

"She doesn't want me to." She poured a Coca-Cola over a glass of ice and sipped it. "She says she'll be all right."

But Julia didn't get better. After a few days, Anjette called a doctor in spite of the older woman's wishes. Dr. O. F. Keen came to the house and found his patient so nauseous she was unable to sleep. Her arms and hands were swollen and she had trouble moving. After examining her, he took Anjette down to the living room for a talk. "That woman needs to be in the hospital."

"I know," she said. "I've tried and tried to get her to go, but she won't. She hated it when she was there last year and doesn't want to go back."

"Well, you better keep trying."

Anjette promised she would.

The household was turned upside down by Julia's illness. Carmen cared for her all day and Anjette and the girls looked after her at night. A week later when Julia finally agreed to be hospitalized, they were all relieved.

"I'll call the doctor while you get her ready, Carmen," Anjette said. "Then you can help me get her to the car."

An hour later, Julia was admitted to Parkview Hospital and taken by wheelchair to a room on the third floor.

The restaurant staff, especially the old-timers, were very fond of Mrs. Lyles. Carrie Jackson who had worked there as a cook for nearly thirty years visited Julia the day after she went into the hospital. It broke her heart to see this woman who had been so full of life lying almost immobile in the bed. The simple act of speaking had become a monumental task.

"It's just terrible," Carrie told Anjette after leaving the room. "I sure hope she gets better soon."

Anjette wasn't optimistic. "I'm afraid she's not going to make it, Carrie. She's so sick."

"Don't say such a thing!"

But Anjette expected the worst.

Anjette hated hospitals—she hated the way they looked, the antiseptic smell of them, even the busy muffled sounds of them. But she knew she was responsible for her mother-in-law. With Julia's only living son, Joseph, in the military and stationed in California, Anjette was the only one who could be there for Julia. She divided her time between the hospital and the restaurant. She had a cot set up in a corner of Julia's room and slept there during the night, depending on her relatives to care for the children.

Cochran, Georgia, was Julia's hometown and several of her relatives still lived there. Three days after her aunt's admission to Parkview, Katharine Gurr read about it in the daily Hospital Admissions column of the *Macon Telegraph*. She called her mother, Nettie Young, immediately.

"Mother, Aunt Julia's in the hospital. I just saw it in the paper!"

The two women drove to Macon that afternoon. It was the Saturday before Labor Day and the town was crowded with shoppers getting ready to send their children back to school. Nettie made her way through the heavy traffic to the hospital.

In Julia's third-floor room, they were shocked by her condition. She looked ten years older than she had a month before. Her skin had a grayish cast and her arms and legs were grossly swollen, making her hands nearly useless. She was unable to lift a glass or press the call button for the nurses.

"The day I was brought in, I tried to pick up a glass," she told her relatives, her voice little more than a whisper, "but I knocked it off the table instead. Now I have to wait for somebody to hold it for me."

They tried their best to cheer her up and appear hopeful, but the two went back to Cochran very worried about Julia.

Severe nausea still plagued Mrs. Lyles and she refused to even try the food in the hospital, so friends and relatives brought different things in an effort to tempt her to eat. Anjette often carried in plates from the restaurant and cajoled her into taking a few bites. Julia had always been partial to chicken pot pie, so the cooks started setting aside a portion of that when it was prepared, hoping she would like it. They made special desserts just for her. Anjette often left the restaurant for the hospital carrying several paper bags of food. And she always took buttermilk.

"She can't keep anything on her stomach except buttermilk," she told the cooks. "I'm going to see that she gets it."

The hospital staff grew familiar with Anjette and she with them. She was there so much of the time she was soon on a first-name basis with many of the employees. Wyolene Poole, Parkview's business manager, was one of the people with whom she'd struck up a casual friendship. On Labor Day, while Julia was napping, Anjette went to see Wyolene. Most of Macon's citizens were taking the holiday off, but in the hospital's business office it was just another day. Wyolene's sister, Evelyn Nutt, had dropped by to see her that afternoon. The two women were chatting when Anjette arrived. Wyolene made the introductions and then asked about Julia.

"It's so sad," Anjette told her. "The doctors think it's some kind of infection, but they can't seem to get her over it. It doesn't look like she's going to live, poor soul, and I guess she knows it." She pulled a folded paper from her purse. "See? She's already making burial arrangements."

She passed the paper to Wyolene, who read it:

> To whom it may concern: In the event of my death, my daughter-in-law, Anjette Donovan Lyles, is to have charge of all funeral arrangements as I have discussed such arrangements with her and she knows my wishes and desires concerning the same. Memorial Chapel is to take charge of my body and is to handle the funeral. This 2nd day of September 1957.

The paper was signed by Julia and witnessed by Anjette. Wyolene shook her head. "The poor thing."

"I know. It's terrible. She can't even get out of bed now. She asked me to come down and get this notarized for her. Can you do it?"

"Why, sure, I can." Wyolene did so and her sister obligingly witnessed it. "Now you let me know if I can do anything for you."

Anjette promised she would.

After Anjette left the office, the two sisters discussed the hard life the widow had led. They had both noticed how worn out she looked and admired her for taking such good care of Julia. It wasn't every woman who would do so much for her former mother-in-law.

Julia's hospital stay stretched into weeks. While the nation's highest court ordered the integration of the Little Rock school system and the National Guard was sent to keep the peace in Arkansas, one middle-aged woman in Macon grew progressively weaker in her fight for life.

Her hospital room was filled with visitors several nights a week and all day Saturdays and Sundays. Friends, relatives and restaurant employees brought flowers, food and small gifts. Katharine and Nettie came often, as did Julia's sister, Nora Bagley. They did their best to stay optimistic and keep the patient's spirits up, but Julia showed no improvement. She had never regained the use of her limbs and was now reduced to using a bed pan and being fed by the nurses. She couldn't turn over or even shift her position in bed without help.

By the last week of September, breathing had become so difficult that oxygen was administered regularly. Her doctors still had not been able to diagnose the cause of her problem. They finally proposed performing a procedure to remove a small portion of her sternum for analysis.

"It might not tell us anything, but it could. And it's the only thing left to do," one of them explained to Anjette.

"But is she strong enough for that?"

He told her he honestly didn't know and Anjette refused to let them do the procedure.

"I don't think she'd live through it. I can't let you do it."

There was no sunrise on September 29. The steady rain that had fallen all night continued as the sky lightened to a leaden gray. Nurse Rubye Lines reported for work on the third floor at seven that morning. The first patient she checked on was Julia Lyles and she found her condition much worse. She was very weak and barely conscious. The doctors who rushed to the room could do nothing more for her.

Anjette didn't leave the hospital all day. When Julia died late that afternoon, only Anjette and Rubye Lines were with her.

CHAPTER FOUR

THE RAIN KEPT FALLING. WHEN JULIA YOUNG LYLES WAS LAID to rest in the churchyard of the Antioch Baptist Church in Cochran, a gray drizzle slowly soaked the mourners and darkened the granite tombstones over her husband and son. Family and friends went back to the house on Pinewood Drive after the service for the usual post-funeral repast of fried chicken, casseroles, deviled eggs and congealed salads. Anjette moved among the guests, speaking to this one and hugging that one. It was becoming a familiar ritual.

One October morning the following week Anjette arrived at the restaurant with Julia's will in her hand.

"I thought she didn't want to get a will," one of the waitresses said.

"She didn't, but I finally talked her into it. And I'm glad I did."

She handed the one-page document around for the others to see. It divided Julia's estate into three equal portions—one third to her son Joseph, one third to Anjette and one third in trust for the "education, support and maintenance" of Carla and Marcia Lyles. Anjette was named executor of the will and trustee for her daughters' portion of the estate. The women gathered around the kitchen table to get a look at it and agreed with their employer that a will certainly made things easier.

On November 4, Anjette presented the will for probate at the Bibb County Courthouse. After Jewell Almond and Mrs. J. B. Bryan testified to witnessing the signature, it was proved and Anjette's appointment as executor was sanctioned.

Meanwhile, life continued. The children attended school and Anjette was able to concentrate on running the restaurant again. Bob Franks still held a place of importance in her life. Business demands kept her from making many trips to be with him now, but when he was out of Macon, hardly a night passed that the two didn't speak by telephone.

He spent several days with her and her daughters at Christmas and Anjette marked the occasion by giving him an expensive watch.

The holidays should have been a happy time for the couple, but Anjette sensed a problem. Franks, who was usually so outgoing and playful, seemed distant and preoccupied. She asked several times if there was a problem, but he always denied this was so. She had to be content with that answer. But the trouble that had simmered under the surface at Christmas finally broke free when in January Franks told her he was seeing another woman.

Anjette was consumed by cold fury, deepened by the knowledge that there was nothing she could do to stop him. She was desperately unhappy and it was a miserable time for those closest to her. She snapped at the staff and her daughters for minor infractions. Her mood was so precarious and her temper so volatile that no one knew what small thing might set her off.

She was desperate to solve her problem. Her dependence on fortune tellers and root doctors increased to the point that she talked to at least one of them every day. Carmen now drove her to the rundown house in Vineville several times a week. Candles were burned at a furious rate at work and at home.

One night in February, she lit a black candle in the restaurant kitchen.

"I heard you only burn them things when you want someone to die," one of the cooks observed.

"Not always," Anjette said placidly. She lifted the candle to reveal a piece of paper on which she'd written the names of Bob Franks and his new girlfriend. "This will break them up. I know it will."

No one disputed it. Agreement was easier than risking an argument.

Preoccupied though she was, Anjette couldn't spend all her time on romantic problems. There was still a business to run and, with her appointment as executor of Mrs. Lyles's will, even more responsibilities than usual. Julia had owned a small, slightly shabby house on Crisp Street. On New Year's Day 1958, Anjette listed it with real estate agent Lewis Smith. It sold in less than a week.

The arrival of March in middle Georgia that year was a soggy event. While there were a few sunny days, rain and fog were the rule. It was on just such a rainy day in early March that Marcia Lyles first became ill. Typical of Sundays, the biggest crowd came to Anjette's early in the afternoon when the churchgoers were released from their devotions and looking for sustenance. Anjette arrived with Carla and Marcia about 11:30 A.M. and stayed through the midday rush. They went home for a rest during the slow afternoon hours, but returned around six that evening. Anjette went straight to the kitchen to oversee dinner preparations.

Mrs. Clifford Webb was the first to notice something was wrong with Marcia. The child was flushed and listless and, when the waitress touched her forehead, it was hot and dry. She went to find Anjette.

"She's got a fever and she's coughing something awful."

Anjette nodded at the familiar symptoms. Marcia had been plagued by respiratory infections all her life. She found her daughter slumped in a booth in the dining room and put a hand across her forehead.

"How do you feel?"

"I'm sick," the child whined, then was seized by a coughing spasm that seemed to come from deep in her chest.

Anjette turned to Mrs. Webb. "Bring me some sugar and a little whiskey."

When the ingredients were at hand, Anjette mixed equal amounts of each in a glass with the ease of someone who'd done it a number of times before. "It's an old-fashioned remedy, but it works."

She stirred it vigorously and gave the mixture to Marcia who gulped it down and then shuddered at the taste as she always did. Anjette returned to the kitchen.

But the whiskey remedy didn't work this time. The child spent the rest of the evening huddled in the booth, coughing frequently. Mrs. Webb checked on her from time to time and brought a cold cloth for her head. Once or twice Marcia went into the kitchen and asked Anjette to take her home, but the restaurant was busy that night and her mother couldn't leave until closing time.

When Anjette took her children home, Marcia was still running a fever and was now shivering with a chill. Once her daughter was in bed, Anjette took her temperature and found it alarmingly high. She immediately called Dr. Keen.

"It sounds like she has a bad case of the flu," he told Anjette. "But with a fever that high, you probably ought to take her on over to the hospital."

Carrie Jackson's telephone rang after midnight. It was Anjette.

"Marcia's in the hospital as sick as she can be," she told her. "She has a fever of 106!"

Carrie struggled to come awake. "What in the world is wrong with her, reckon?"

"They think it's the Asiatic flu."

Carrie assured Anjette that she would handle the opening of the restaurant the next morning and promised to stop by the hospital after she got off work.

By morning, Marcia's temperature had dropped several degrees. Nurse Leila Radlein told her mother she appeared to have an acute respiratory infection, but was already responding well to treatment. They didn't consider her condition serious and Anjette felt she could leave long enough to make a quick visit to the restaurant. After bringing the staff up to date on Marcia's condition and satisfying herself that the place was running fine without her, she fixed a plate of food and a glass of tea for her daughter and returned to the hospital.

The nursing staff at Parkview found Marcia Lyles to be a difficult patient. She cried easily and had to be cajoled or threatened to take medicine by mouth. The worst came when she had to be given an injection. Since she was on a regimen of strong antibiotics, shots were necessary several times a day and each time it was an ordeal for both the patient and the staff. The child screamed and fought so hard that the procedure took three nurses—two to hold her down and one to administer the hypodermic.

Marcia's condition steadily improved. After only a couple of days, she began calling Carmen Howard every afternoon to ask if any of her friends had come by or if she had received any mail. She called the restaurant as well and the staff was cheered by how energetic she sounded. By Wednesday, she was so much better that the nurses expected her to go home by the weekend.

Anjette called Fannie Butts at the restaurant.

"Marcia wants you to come and see her when you get off work."

"Why, sure," Fannie said. "You tell her I'll be there."

A cook at the restaurant for years, Fannie had known Marcia since she was a baby and regarded her as family. She was happy to take the time to visit the hospital and flattered that Marcia had asked for her.

It was nearly dark when Fannie got to Parkview Hospital. There were already visitors in Marcia's room. Her aunt and grandmother were chatting with Anjette as Fannie made her way to the bed and leaned over for a hug. Marcia immediately launched into a description of the hospital and her stay there. As the girl chattered away, Fannie could see that she was still not well. She looked tired, her face was flushed and the hug revealed that she was still running a fever, but she was also alert, talkative and in high spirits—a welcome change from her condition Sunday night. She didn't seem any sicker than other people Fannie had known with bronchitis or similar ailments. The cook was feeling cheerful when she left the room. But Anjette didn't share her optimism. She followed Fannie into the corridor.

"What do you think about Marcia?" she asked nervously. "You think she's going to get well?"

"Look to me like she will."

Anjette lowered her voice. "I think she's going to die."

"No, she be fine," Fannie told her. She knew Anjette had seen too many people close to her die. "All sickness isn't death."

But Fannie's reassurance didn't help, nor did that of the doctors. Anjette became preoccupied with the idea Marcia was going to die.

She stopped Bessie Treace in the hall one day. "Come and look at her legs," she asked in an eerie echo of the request she'd made three years before when Buddy Gabbert lay in the same hospital room. The nurse did as she asked and saw that the child's legs were darker than the rest of her body. She couldn't think of anything to say to her mother.

There were visitors to Marcia's room every afternoon. Relatives and friends crowded in to see her, bringing flowers and good wishes. The little girls in her Brownie troop made get-well cards and sent them to her. Everyone was confident she would recover—everyone except Anjette. She continued to fret, morbidly convinced the child would die. As she had when Mrs. Lyles was ill, Anjette had a cot put in the room for herself. She spent every minute she could at the hospital and regularly brought her daughter food and drinks.

"You know, there's no need for you to bring drinks to her," Leila Radlein told Anjette one afternoon when she'd brought Marcia a glass of lemonade. "Every floor of the hospital has a kitchen. We can provide anything you need here."

But Anjette didn't want the hospital staff doing it for her. It was important to her that she prepare Marcia's treats herself.

Marcia's recovery wasn't as complete as the doctors hoped. The cough lingered and her temperature never returned to normal, so they kept her there in Parkview where they could monitor her condition closely. When she'd been hospitalized for a week, Carrie Jackson visited. Afterwards, she sat down in the waiting room with Anjette.

"Marcia's going to die, Carrie. I know it."

"I don't know why you'd think such a thing. She's doing fine."

But Anjette would not be comforted. "I've been thinking about her funeral. You know, she sings in the children's choir at church. I'm going to have them sing at her funeral."

Carrie tried, but couldn't make her see things more sensibly. No one, it seemed, could free Anjette of the dreadful certainty her child was going to die. She seemed convinced that she was afflicted with some sort of curse and that all those people close to her would die, one after another, leaving her completely alone.

Early the next week, a letter was delivered to Nora Bagley in Cochran. It read:

Please come at once. She's getting the
same dose as the others. Please come at once.

There was no signature and Nora didn't understand what it meant. However, when a second similar letter came a few days later, she consulted with other relatives. The letters seemed to warn that Marcia Lyles was in danger. They debated over what to do and eventually went to Macon where they talked with an investigator with the Sheriff's Office and a member of the Solicitor's staff. Lester Chapman, the Bibb County Coroner, was called and consulted. The men finally decided that the accusations were so vague there was no need to follow up on them. The letters were probably just a spiteful attempt to stir up trouble.

Marcia's condition now began to worsen. The mottled, bluish discoloration Bessie Treace had seen on her legs spread and covered her back and chest and she was nauseated most of the time. Anjette tried to find things her daughter might want to eat or drink. Several times she sent restaurant employees up the street to the Capitol Theater for a grape soda, the kind Marcia particularly liked, and had them bring it to her at the hospital. But the effort was wasted. Marcia could barely swallow.

One night after the child had been there about two weeks, the quiet of the hospital was split by a long, terrified shriek. Nurses who ran to Marcia's room found her thrashing wildly about while Anjette desperately tried to hold her on the bed.

"Get them off me!" the child screamed, slapping at her body. "The bugs, get them off me!"

They couldn't calm her and, after a short time, administered a sedative. She soon drifted into a fitful sleep.

The doctors originally blamed the outburst on a particularly vivid nightmare, but the terrifying hallucinations became regular occurrences. At one time, Marcia believed there was a bee on her arm and tearfully begged the nurses to get it off. Another time she was convinced that her hand was falling off. During these episodes, she fought and screamed, desperate to escape the imaginary horrors. She had to be restrained to prevent her from injuring herself. The nurses, in turn, were consumed with pity for her and exhausted by the physical struggles necessary to keep her in bed. Marcia was kept sedated most of the time now.

Dr. Keen grew increasingly frustrated by the lack of progress in the case. On March 12, he called Dr. Robert Ireland, an internist, in for consultation. Ireland stopped by the hospital that night on his way home and, after examining Marcia, called his nurse.

"I want you to cancel my morning appointments," he told her. "I'll be here at the hospital. This is a very sick child."

Ireland spent most of the next several days with her. He went over her records time and again and quizzed her mother and the doctors and nurses who had been treating her, searching for any clue to the cause of her illness, but no diagnosis presented itself.

Marcia lay in the hospital through the month of March, the cause of her condition a mystery. Dr. Ireland became more and more uneasy as the days passed. Although he never voiced his suspicions, he began to wonder if Marcia's condition could be the result of some outside element. He finally ordered that she receive food, drink or medicine only from the nurses attending her.

As the month drew to an end, the little girl suddenly began to fail. Huddled in the big bed, surrounded by an oxygen tent, she appeared very small and helpless. She struggled for each breath. She pleaded with the nurses or her mother to turn the oxygen up and, although they complied, doing so didn't help. It appeared possible that Anjette's gloomy prediction was going to come true.

"She'll soon be going home to Little Ben and her grandmother," Anjette told the restaurant employees one morning.

This was too much for Fannie Butts, who burst into tears and ran into the restroom, crying for the child she'd known and loved since she was a baby.

On Friday evening, April 4, Anjette, her sister-in-law Alice Donovan and her mother gathered around the bed as Marcia, now unconscious, struggled to breathe. A nurse hovered nearby. One last tortured breath was drawn and released and then there were no more. The nurse checked vital signs and then turned off the oxygen. The only sound in the room was quiet sobbing. Marcia Lyles was dead, three months short of her tenth birthday.

Robert Ireland's initial reaction to Marcia's death was anger. She'd been so young and he'd worked so hard to help her. The nature of her illness was still uncertain, and the man who had fought for nearly a month to save her was determined to learn the cause of her death. Within an hour of her death, he called the Bibb County Medical Director.

"I want you to perform an autopsy," he said.

Dr. L. H. Campbell agreed to perform the procedure. Around midnight he went to the hospital where he conducted a standard postmortem examination of Marcia Lyles, taking minute organ sections and tissue samples for microscopic examination. From what he already knew of the case, he was nearly certain death was due to a respiratory infection of some kind. But when he examined the specimens through the microscope the next day, he saw nothing out of the ordinary. He couldn't believe it. He'd been so sure of what he would find. He looked at the slides again and again, but still found nothing to indicate the cause of death. He stared at the magnified images for so long that his vision blurred and he began to see specks that weren't there.

Anjette had stayed at Marcia's bedside most of the time she'd been sick, so Carla's aunt and uncle had been caring for her. While it was initially unsettling to move from one house to another, she'd adapted quickly. What was a disruptive situation for the adults around her soon became routine to the six year old girl. School occupied much of her time and she was as much at home with her grandmother or her aunt and uncle as she was at the Pinewood Drive house. She knew Marcia was ill, of course, but since everyone told her so, she expected her sister would be coming home soon. She was completely unprepared when they took her back to her own house Saturday morning and an exhausted Anjette broke the news.

"Marcia won't be with us anymore, Carla. She's gone to be with God."

Carla looked from her mother to Carmen and back to her mother, searching for more explanation. Then, as the meaning of the words registered, she screamed, ran from the room and sank to the floor behind the hall door, sobbing.

Later that day, Anjette and Carmen drove to the Memorial Chapel Funeral Home where visitation would be held that evening. Marcia lay in a small casket, dressed in her Sunday best. Anjette reached out to touch her face. "Isn't she pretty?" she asked.

Then she gently placed a bride doll and a small white Bible into the casket with her oldest daughter.

CHAPTER FIVE

WHEN LESTER CHAPMAN, THE COUNTY CORONER, HEARD about Marcia's death Saturday afternoon, and his first thought was of the anonymous letters he'd dismissed as too vague to warrant any action. Now the possibility that there had been some substance to the warnings couldn't be ignored. He called Dr. Campbell.

"I think you should perform an autopsy on that child."

"I already did, Lester. I couldn't find a thing."

But when Chapman explained the background of the case and raised the possibility of poisoning, the medical examiner agreed to a more extensive examination.

At 4:00 A.M. Sunday morning, only hours before the local churches would celebrate Easter with singing and the ringing of bells, Dr. Campbell let himself into the Memorial Chapel Funeral Home and made his way along the silent hallways to the room where Marcia Lyles lay. He had intentionally scheduled his visit for this hour to avoid any encounter with the family or visitors. He took Marcia from her casket, carefully removed her frilly dress and opened the small body for a second time. This time he took larger amounts of tissue from the kidneys and liver and snipped several pieces of hair from the back of her head to accommodate the toxicology tests. As an afterthought, he took a sample of the Velva-Glo embalming fluid used by the undertaker. Each specimen was placed in an individual pint fruit jar, which he had washed out and sterilized for just this purpose. He screwed the caps down tight, wrapped the tops with masking tape and initialed the overlaps. When he left the funeral home the sun had already risen.

The position of Bibb County Medical Examiner didn't come with a nicely equipped laboratory. Campbell worked out of his medical office, and sometimes his home, and had learned to make do with what he had. He stored Marcia Lyles's tissue samples in the only refrigerated equipment available to him—his own kitchen refrigerator.

The funeral service for the oldest Lyles daughter was held at Memorial Chapel. Then a small procession of cars set out for the two-hour drive to the tiny east Georgia town of Wadley. They wound through rolling hills, past rivers lined with moss-hung trees. Along the way, cars pulled off the road to let them pass. In the small towns, people on the sidewalks stopped to watch the sad procession and men quickly took off their hats. Between two freshly plowed fields, the hearse turned onto a dirt road and the other cars followed, dust billowing behind them. The road ended at Coleman's Chapel, a little white clapboard Methodist church. A variety of tombstones spread out to the left, ending at a line of trees.

The mourners got out of the cars and made their way to the Watkins family plot, which was set off from the rest of the churchyard by a small iron fence. Jetta Donovan had been a Watkins before her marriage. Marcia Lyles was laid to rest near her grandfather, William Donovan.

After the last graveside prayer was said, most of those who'd gathered for the service walked slowly back to their cars, but Anjette lagged behind to speak with A. R. King, who had handled the service and burial for Memorial Chapel.

"Mr. King, I've been thinking about it a lot and I believe that Marcia's father should be buried beside her. Can you take care of that for me?"

King assured her he could. Arrangements were made then and there, and a few days later, Ben Lyles's body was disinterred from the churchyard in Cochran and reburied beside his daughter in Coleman's Chapel Cemetery. No ceremony marked the occasion

Anjette couldn't seem to dismiss the possibility of more misfortune coming her way. A couple of days after the funeral, she confessed to one of her employees that she was worried about Carla.

"She said she wants to go to heaven to be with Marcia. I don't know what to do with her."

"Time will take care of it, Anjette. It just takes time."

Talk spreads like kudzu in a small town. While the authorities did their best to be discreet, word was bound to leak out. Overnight, whispers about anonymous letters and autopsies sprung up. People spoke the word "poison" behind their hands.

Anjette was trying hard to regain some normalcy in her life. If she noticed any new interest in her or was aware of eyes that watched and then were quickly averted, she never showed it. But one morning, less than a week after Marcia's death, she was forced to confront the gossip. Butch Allen, a regular customer, came to see her.

"Anjette, I think you should know that people are talking. They're saying Marcia was poisoned and that you did it," he said with the self-assurance of someone doing something for the other person's own good.

For a moment, she stared at him, as her world rocked on its foundations.

"How could anyone believe that?" she asked finally. "I would not hurt my own child!"

Allen couldn't provide any details, and left the restaurant a little later. But Anjette couldn't stop thinking about what he'd said. Mrs. Webb was taking a break, sipping coffee and reading the morning paper in a booth, when Anjette joined her.

"Before Marcia got sick, Carmen said she saw her and Carla and the Jones children playing doctor and they had some Ant Terro poison. She took it away from them, but now I wonder if that could be what made Marcia sick."

"Ant Terro? Gosh, Anjette, don't you have a thing like that put out of the children's reach?"

"Sure I do. I had it up in a closet, but I guess she climbed up and got it."

Leonard Campbell had also heard the talk, but he didn't believe the rumors. He had grown to admire Anjette and couldn't conceive of her, or any mother, harming her own child. But he still continued to puzzle over the case, frustrated by his inability to pinpoint the cause of death.

A week after the funeral, he called Anjette and asked her to come to his office. There were three reasons for the invitation: he wanted to go over Marcia's medical history with her once again to satisfy himself he hadn't overlooked anything; and he believed that, in fairness, Anjette should be told about the gossip being spread about her. He had grown to like this forthright woman and he detested gossip. He also felt he owed her the courtesy of telling her he would be sending the tissue samples from her daughter's body to the crime lab in Atlanta for toxicology tests. That, he hoped, would settle once and for all the cause of the child's death.

Anjette sat quietly in Campbell's office, hands folded in her lap, as he related all this to her. Hearing the ugly rumors from someone as prominent as Dr. Campbell was a shock. She considered telling him about the children playing with the ant poison, but decided against it. In the end, she just thanked him for his concern.

All that night she struggled with the question of what she should do and by morning she had decided Campbell ought to be told. She went to his office again, that afternoon this time accompanied by a shy Carla. Once inside the door, she set a brown paper bag on his desk.

"Carla has something to tell you, Dr. Campbell." She nodded at the child.

"Me and the Jones twins," the little girl stammered, "We were playing doctor..." She looked at her mother, "...with some bottles."

Anjette indicated the paper bag. Campbell looked inside and found two partially full bottles of Terro ant poison.

"I think Marcia may have played with the same bottles."

"My God!" the doctor said.

He hurried to pick up Carla and set her on an examining table. While he checked her vital signs and looked for any evidence of poisoning, he kept up a running interrogation.

"How do you feel, Carla? Have you been sick? A tummy ache, maybe? Let me look in your mouth."

When he had determined to his own satisfaction that she was fine, he turned his attention to Anjette.

"She's all right. How are the twins? Have you talked to their mother?"

Looking confused, Anjette confessed she hadn't thought about calling her.

"Well, maybe you should call her now," Campbell suggested a bit impatiently. "This is serious."

Anjette agreed and asked for a telephone book. She flipped through the pages, found the number she wanted and dialed.

"Mrs. Jones? This is Anjette Lyles. I'm here in Dr. Campbell's office and I've just found out that the children might have gotten into some poison. I think it's all right. Carla is fine. But you might want to take the girls to the doctor."

She listened for a moment. "Okay. Well, I just wanted to let you know."

She hung up and turned to Campbell. "She said they're fine, but she'll keep an eye on them just in case."

Campbell kept the bottles of ant poison Anjette had brought in. He sealed and marked them, and on April 11 sent them, along with Marcia's tissue samples and the embalming fluid, to the crime lab by Railway Express.

On April 17, Dr. Larry Howard of the Georgia State Crime Laboratory notified Campbell and Coroner Lester Chapman that the tissue samples he'd analyzed were positive for the presence of arsenic. Within hours of receiving the news, the coroner met with Sheriff James Wood and Bibb County Solicitor General William West. What had begun as mere suspicion was now a full-fledged homicide investigation.

Anjette was becoming frightened. She consulted William K. Buffington, a local attorney, and told him about the rumors. Among other things, she told him, she was concerned she might be blamed for leaving the poison within reach of the children. Buffington listened to her story and counseled patience.

"There's nothing we can do but wait. It may be that nothing comes of this at all and you've worried yourself sick for no reason."

Anjette had to be content with that.

That Sunday, Anjette attended church at Mulberry Street Methodist. By the time the service was over, she knew she was ill. She was running a fever and a familiar pain throbbed in her right leg and side. By early evening, she'd been admitted to Parkview Hospital for treatment of phlebitis. Coincidentally, she was put in the same third floor room where Buddy, Julia and Marcia had all been patients. Dr. Robert Ireland was her attending physician.

Like other people in town, J. Taylor Phillips had heard the rumors about Marcia's death and, for several days now, had been aware of speculation that Anjette was going to be arrested. Reasoning that, if he had been in her place, he'd want to be told what was happening, he went to see her.

There was no way to be subtle about it. "Anjette, I think some murder warrants are going to be taken for you."

"Is this about Marcia?"

"Yes, I'm afraid so."

"But I didn't do anything. My maid saw her drinking ant poison and that's probably the way the poison got into her blood. It wasn't *my* fault!"

"It's more than that. They've been bringing witnesses into the Sheriff's Office. Mrs. Lyles's relatives, I think. They must be looking into her death as well as Marcia's."

She was quiet for a minute, getting herself under control. She knew she had to be strong. When her heart rate had slowed, she turned back to her visitor. "Would you hand me my purse from the table there?"

She opened the bag, removed a piece of paper and handed Phillips a photostat of a letter. It read,

Anjette,
Please forgive me for doing the things to
you that I did and to Little Ben. I did wrong
and for that I am paying with my death as I
am the cause of my son's death and my own.
I know I was sick and you did all you could to
make me well. My own family will do nothing
for me.
Love,
Julia Y. Lyles

She waited until he'd read it, then said, "My maid Carmen found that in one of Mrs. Lyles's pocketbooks at the house. I thought I should make a copy of it. You can see that it shows I had nothing to do with her death or Little Ben's."

Meanwhile, investigators were gathering as much information about Anjette and the deaths of the four people closest to her as they could. Interviews were conducted with her relatives and friends. Every employee of Anjette's Restaurant was called to the courthouse for interviews. Rosemary Reynolds was at home when word came she was wanted at the courthouse. She walked several miles there in the hot sun and was then kept waiting on a hard bench in the corridor for hours until it was her turn to be interrogated.

After all the interviews were over, the investigative team met to compare notes. They drew the conclusion that they had enough information to move forward. On April 24, a petition was filed in

Jefferson County Superior Court requesting permission to disinter the body of Ben Lyles for the purpose of postmortem examination. Leonard Campbell was the petitioner. Judge R. N. Humphrey granted authority for the exhumation. A similar request was filed the next day in Bleckley County to exhume Julia Lyles's body. Permission was granted there by Judge John Whaley.

Spring is the season of storms in Georgia. Warm moist air pours up from the Gulf of Mexico and collides with the lingering cold drifting down from the country's midsection to produce some memorable weather. April 28, the day chosen to disinter both bodies, dawned cloudy, warm and close; just the sort of conditions that could produce bad storms.

Six people set out from Macon for Wadley. Adam Greene from the Solicitor's Office accompanied Dr. Campbell and Coroner Chapman. Dr. Larry Howard, along with his wife who acted as his assistant, had driven down from Atlanta to join them. Rounding out the group was David Banks, a young Macon police officer who had known Julia and Ben well. He'd been asked to go along to make positive identification of the bodies.

A. R. King met them in Wadley and had his workers excavate the grave in Coleman Chapel Cemetery where he had so recently reburied the body of Ben Lyles, Jr. There hadn't even been time for grass to grow over the grave. The heavy vault was dragged out of the ground with pulleys and the seal broken. Then the casket itself was opened, revealing the gruesome sight inside. Before anything was disturbed, Howard carefully photographed the corpse.

"Officer Banks," Howard called when he had finished, "come over here and see if you can identify this man."

Banks approached the grave hesitantly. While he'd seen dead bodies, this was the first time he would see one that had been dead for years. He looked inside the casket and recognized Ben Lyles, Jr., at least he recognized his profile from the nose up. That part of his face was relatively well preserved. The lower portion of his chin and neck had deteriorated badly.

"That's Ben Lyles," he told them, his voice unsteady. "If I'm not badly mistaken, he'll be wearing a ring with his initials engraved on it."

Campbell and Howard located the ring and began carefully removing it from the decayed finger. This was too much for Banks. He hurried away from the open grave. As he vomited on the grass at the side of the cemetery, he heard someone reading the initials aloud.

Assisted by Mrs. Howard and Dr. Campbell, Dr. Howard performed an abbreviated autopsy on Ben Lyles, Jr. there in the churchyard, removing sections of organs as well as a hank of hair. The samples were placed in small bottles, sealed, marked, and stored in his bag for transport back to Atlanta.

They left King to rebury Ben and drove southwest to Bleckley County where Julia Lyles was buried at Antioch Baptist Church. As the day wore on, violent thunderstorms erupted. High winds tore through the middle of the state, driving hail and drenching rain before them. A freak dust storm struck Bleckley County. Dr. Campbell and the others had to work around the turbulent weather, sheltering from the worst of it in their vehicles. This time the ordeal of opening the casket was easier for Banks. Except for some scattered mold, Julia's body was in good condition and she was easily recognized. The officer again made the official identification. The body was quickly photographed and Dr. Howard retrieved the necessary samples as the wind whipped the nearby trees and thunder rumbled in the distance.

The investigators had determined that an autopsy had been performed on Buddy Gabbert at the Veterans Hospital in Dublin. Tissue samples had been taken and stored there, but no toxicology tests had ever been run. Arrangements were quickly made to have Gabbert's tissue samples delivered to Atlanta.

Only a few days later, Howard called with the not unexpected news that both Julia's and Ben's bodies contained arsenic. The tissue samples from the Veterans Hospital were also positive for arsenic. It was his opinion that in all of the cases poison, administered in small doses over several weeks or months had been the cause of death.

CHAPTER SIX

"FOUL PLAY SUSPECTED IN 2 DEATHS" WAS THE *MACON Telegraph*'s front page headline the next morning. The exhumation of Ben and Julia Lyles's bodies was detailed in the accompanying story. The nurse who brought Anjette's breakfast brought her a newspaper as well, then puttered around the room, glancing at the patient from time to time to catch her reaction. Her dawdling was wasted. Anjette scanned the front page, then set the paper aside and began calmly eating her breakfast. She was well aware of the nurse's interest and she was not going to give her the satisfaction of reacting to the news even though her heart was pounding in her chest.

Macon was ordinarily a quiet town where murder was something that happened in far away places. But even at the beginning, the Lyles case had all the indications of becoming a huge story. Reporters from both of the town's newspapers hovered anxiously in the courthouse hallways all morning, hoping for an official statement, but Solicitor General William West flatly refused discuss the investigation. The Sheriff was similarly unwilling to talk. The reporters had no choice but to wait for further developments.

Late that morning, Anjette's doctor came to her room and announced she was being moved to Macon Hospital.

"I don't understand," she said. "Why?"

"Have you seen the paper?"

She had.

"Well, so has everyone else. The telephones haven't stopped ringing all morning. The whole town is calling here to ask you questions or ask questions about you. And there are already reporters in the lobby. It's just a matter of time before one of them manages to sneak in here."

An hour later the staff slipped her out the back door, and shortly afterward she settled into a room on the fifth floor of Macon Hospital with a NO VISITORS sign hung prominently on the door. She called William Buffington, hoping for some encouraging news, but all he did was order her not to talk to anyone about the suspect deaths.

"All we can do now is wait," he told her. That statement was becoming a monotonous refrain.

Tuesday, May 6, was unusually cool. People pulled out the sweaters and jackets they'd already put away for the year and didn't linger outside in the chill wind. But Lester Chapman, Solicitor General West, Sheriff Wood and the investigators working on the Lyles case hardly noticed the change in weather. They spent the entire day closeted in the Sheriff's courthouse office. Their only concern was the question of whether they had enough evidence to charge the pretty widow with murder. They examined every witness's statement and took turns trying to pick them apart. They made a list of reasons to charge her and compared it with a list of reasons not to do so. They drank gallons of coffee and the air grew so thick with cigarette smoke they had to open windows for ventilation. Finally about 4:00 P.M. the decision was made. The men cleared out of the room and Lester Chapman went directly to a judge and swore out warrants charging Anjette Lyles with four counts of murder. Minutes later, the warrants were handed over to Sheriff Wood for service.

For the first time, Wood was forced to consider the practicalities associated with arresting Anjette. Arrests of women, especially white women, were unusual and he knew that this case would attract a lot of attention. Everything had to be handled properly. While women might have made some small inroads into law enforcement in the big cities, there were no female deputies in the Bibb County Sheriff's Department. However, this day a woman's presence was necessary. There would be no skimping on propriety. So Sheriff Wood enlisted his secretary, Latrelle West, to accompany him and Deputy John Gibson to Macon Hospital.

When Gibson, Wood and Latrelle West walked into Anjette's hospital room at five that afternoon, her usual smiling greeting was answered with stony expressions. Wood held a handful of folded papers out to her. "Anjette Lyles, you're under arrest for the murders of Ben Lyles, Joe Neal Gabbert, Julia Lyles and Marcia Lyles."

There was nothing to say. She'd lived with the fear this day might come, but she'd never really believed it would. Now these people, people she *knew*, were standing here, staring at her like they'd never seen her before and accusing her of the most vile crimes imaginable.

Sheriff Wood spoke briefly with the doctors about the advisability of taking his prisoner to the jail. They convinced him Anjette should remain in the hospital until her health permitted moving her. Wood agreed, but arranged for a deputy to be stationed outside her door twenty-four hours a day. She would not be left alone again until they had locked her in a cell. Latrelle West was selected to stay in the room with her that night.

The door closed behind the lawmen and Anjette and Latrelle looked at each other, exchanging tentative smiles. They weren't exactly strangers. They'd been casual acquaintances for years and Latrelle had gone to high school with one of Anjette's brothers. Still, she was uncomfortable guarding a prisoner—which is how she thought of what she was doing. It was a far cry from the typing, filing and answering telephones that were her normal duties. But Anjette had made her living for years making people feel at home and that's just what she did that evening. In the glow of Anjette's personality, Latrelle relaxed and found that conversation came easily. In only a little while, they were joking and laughing like people making small talk at a party. The time passed quickly as they shared opinions of clothes and men, sometimes giggling like school girls. Eventually the talk turned to the murder case.

"What I don't understand is why they're picking on *me*," Anjette said. "I sure didn't get anything from them dying. Not a thing. And I don't know how anyone could think I'd hurt Marcia." She grew silent for a moment and Latrelle thought Anjette might cry, but then she rallied. "But it's going to be all right. I know it is. They can't really do anything to me because I didn't do it. I have a letter that will clear up all these charges."

"A letter?"

She gave a short, definitive nod. "That's right. It's in Mrs. Lyles's handwriting and it will burn 'em up." She took a deep breath. "Besides, all the brass hats in Macon will be behind me. I know all of them. They won't let this happen."

Two visitors came to the hospital room that evening. Dr. Ireland was there first to check his patient's vital signs and ask how she was feeling. His visit lasted only a few minutes. Then, around 10:00 P.M., William Buffington arrived.

"I'm sorry I wasn't here earlier," he told her. "I knew there had been in an arrest, but I had to be over in Harris County. I got back as soon as I could."

He moved to position himself between the bed and the chair where Latrelle West sat. When he spoke, his voice was very low and Latrelle had to strain to hear what he said.

"Are you okay? Have they treated you all right?"

"Yes, I'm fine."

"I talked to the reporters outside tonight."

"There are reporters *here*?" she asked.

"Yeah, I expect they'll be here all night. When I talked to them, I told them you said 'I have committed no crime'. And that's the only comment I want you to make to any reporters from now on. Do you understand? You're to say, 'I have committed no crime'."

She nodded, her eyes never leaving his face. He hoped she was paying close attention. Over the years, he'd spent a lot of time trying to undo the damage his clients had done by talking out of turn. Buffington intended to keep that from happening in this case.

He left, promising to call her the next day.

Anjette was too worked up to sleep. She and Latrelle were still talking when Polly McDaniel, wife of one of the deputies, showed up about 11:00 P.M.

"The Sheriff sent me to relieve you, Latrelle."

She had brought coffee in cardboard cups and the three sipped the hot drinks and talked of people they knew, the weather and any other innocuous topic that arose. But there was no more talk about murders.

Latrelle left just before midnight and Mrs. McDaniel dimmed the lights in the room. Anjette finally relaxed enough to sleep.

Earlier that evening, Rosemary Reynolds had been relaxing in her home across the river when a news bulletin interrupted the program on her television. She listened, amazed, as a man calmly announced Anjette Lyles had been arrested on four counts of murder. Even though she knew the deaths were being investigated, Rosemary was shaken by the news. She was glad she'd been sitting down when she heard it.

A sensational headline greeted Maconites Wednesday morning. "Macon Woman Held In Deaths" was the banner across the top of the front page. In smaller letters was "Cafe Owner is Accused of Slayings." The story in which Anjette was described as the "attractive, silver-haired widow" recounted the events leading up to the arrest and the arrest itself. A final short paragraph informed readers that Carla had been placed in the "custody and protection" of the Juvenile Court.

A ten-year old photograph of Anjette with short dark hair, looking somewhat theatrical in a photographer's drape, held a place of prominence just below the headline. A much smaller photo of Marcia showed a pudgy school girl smiling shyly at the camera.

The press was already obsessed with the story. Reporters waited outside the hospital and in the courthouse corridors, alert for any crumb of news. Late that afternoon, a reporter from the *Macon Telegraph* strolled into the hospital lobby and nonchalantly made his way up to the fifth floor. He loitered in the hallway until staff members spotted him and asked him to leave. He returned to the lobby, but only a few minutes passed before he slipped back upstairs where he lingered near the nurses' station and managed to overhear that Anjette was "running a temperature" before hurrying away to avoid the police officer the nurses had called to remove him. This non-event rated a small box of its own on the front page of the next day's paper.

It was already dark Wednesday night when there was a loud knock at Carmen Howard's door. She found four sheriff's deputies standing on her front porch.

"Do you have a key to Anjette Lyles's house, Carmen?" one asked her. She'd never seen this man before, and he didn't bother to introduce himself.

"Yes, sir, I do."

"Then go get it and come with us. We've got a warrant to search the place."

"Why I got to come? I don't have anything to do with this."

But arguing was pointless and Carmen knew it. If the police wanted you to go with them, you went. Minutes later, she was in the back seat of one of the two unmarked sheriff's cars. At the Pinewood Drive house, she unlocked the front door, then stood out of the way as they searched, speaking only when she was asked which bedroom was whose.

The house was a typical suburban split-level with comfortable, but unremarkable furniture. The few children's toys scattered around were sad reminders of the little girls who had lived there. Ballet dancers painted on the staircase wall leading up to the bedrooms, positioned so the figures seemed to dance up the steps, added an odd touch of whimsy to the occasion.

They searched quickly and seized some financial papers, tins of ant poison, rolls of negatives and other items from Anjette's bedroom. But they were distracted from their searching for a few minutes by the evidence of Anjette's dabbling in the occult.

"Hey," one of the deputies shouted, "ya'll come here and look at this stuff!"

None of the search team had ever seen such things before—a tin containing love powder incense, a box of good luck powder, scented salt for sprinkling around the house, a bottle labeled love potion, strange looking roots in bottles of oil, and of course, numerous candles. They examined it all, picking up the bottles and smelling some of the contents, but interesting though it was, it didn't seem to have any connection to the case. They left it all behind.

Carmen was returned home, but the officers kept the house key.

When the investigators met early Wednesday morning to consider what they had taken in their search and what had been left behind, the items that Sheriff Wood was now calling "voodoo material" were discussed at some length.

"I think you should have brought those thing in," the Sheriff said.

"But it was only candles and powders. It didn't have anything to do with the killings."

"We don't know that yet."

So the deputies returned to the house and conducted a second search. This time, everything that could have any conceivable bearing on the case, including all the occult items, was boxed up and carried back to the courthouse.

That evening Sheriff Wood held a press conference and displayed a few of the more sensational items taken from Anjette's house. The press loved it. Vice-President Richard Nixon was touring South America at the time. During an anti-American demonstration in Peru, he had been struck by a rock. But the Vice-President rated only a few paragraphs below the Lyles story Thursday morning. The day's headline was

"Voodoo Material Is Found In Lyles Home". Photographs of love powders and black candles were arranged across the top of the page.

On Friday morning, Dr. Ireland examined Anjette and pronounced her well enough to leave the hospital.

"Does that mean I'm going to jail?" she asked, a faint tremor in her voice.

"I'm afraid so," Ireland told her.

By 1:30, William Buffington was at the hospital, trying to convince his client that the situation wasn't as terrible as it seemed.

"It's not as bad you think it's going to be. They won't mistreat you there."

She nodded, but didn't speak. How could he know how bad it was in jail? He wasn't the one who was to be locked up.

At 2:00 P.M., deputies John Gibson and Billy Murphy arrived. They wheeled Anjette, blinking in the bright sun, out of Macon Hospital and helped her into an unmarked car. The wheelchair was folded and stored in the trunk. They chatted during the short ride, and the prisoner even laughed a couple of times. Near the rear door of the courthouse, groups of people had started gathering as soon as word of the move got out. By the time Anjette arrived, nearly three hundred people were waiting on the street to get a glimpse of her. Workers in nearby office buildings crowded in the windows overlooking the scene.

Anjette emptied her face of all expression when she got out of the car and took her seat in the wheelchair. They wheeled her quickly through the back door and into the basement hallway as flashbulbs exploded around them. She could hardly see by the time the elevator doors closed.

The Bibb County Jail was located on the top floor of the courthouse and Anjette was given a cell by herself. She hardly had time to take in her surroundings—a twelve by twelve room holding a cot and a toilet, with bars across one wall—before an investigator showed up. Harry Harris stayed in her cell for several hours, interrogating her about the case, even though she was adamant that she knew nothing about any poisonings. She told him over and over that she hadn't killed anyone or benefited from anyone's death.

"If you're telling the truth," he finally told her, "it will be all right. But if you're not, we will find out."

Anjette spent the night alone in her cell, trying not to lose her nerve, but it was difficult lying in the darkness, wondering if anyone would believe her.

Sheriff Wood held another press conference on May 10 where he announced that as a result of the four deaths, Anjette had received between $40,000 and $50,000 in inheritances and insurance benefits. He also revealed that they had found ant poison in her home and that they had witnesses who saw her prepare liquids that were taken to both Marcia and Julia.

"We can actually prove that she administered all these liquids to all the victims," he said. "Evidence is increasing and will be considerably stronger by the time any trial is held."

William Buffington had already arranged for Jack Gautier and Roy Rhodenhiser to share the defense duties with him, and the newly formed defense team took strong exception to Sheriff Wood's published comments. Within hours of his press conference, they issued a written response.

"If Sheriff Wood made the comments attributed to him, he is invading the province of the court and jury. We wonder if Mr. Wood is endeavoring to try his case in the forums of the newspapers, radio and television in lieu of a court of law."

The statement also contained an update on Anjette's condition. "Mrs. Lyles is resting comfortably, considering the fact that she has a serious physical disability and is under the care of a physician. We also wish to report that our client, Mrs. Anjette Lyles, has stated to us 'I have committed no crime.'"

The Lyles case was becoming the murder case of the decade. Any new information, no matter how insignificant, was published. When there was nothing new to report, the media rehashed what had already been reported. And the local press were not alone in their fascination with the case. The *New York Daily News* picked up the story on the wire and ran with it. On May 10 they scooped the Macon papers by printing a copyrighted interview with Bob Franks.

The pilot, interviewed in his Nashville, Tennessee, home, told their reporter that he had dated Anjette and described her as "very attractive and affectionate. I thought she was a very fine person. When I heard the news from Macon, it floored me. I damn near fell out of my chair."

But some of his comments were less flattering. "At pretty well every hotel I stayed as I flew around, she would telephone me, even overseas. I never accepted any of her calls. I don't even know how she knew where to find me. We started dating, going to nightclubs and places. I got the idea she was looking for another husband. In fact, it was pretty obvious. But I don't know if she picked me. We never discussed matrimony."

The *Daily News* story was picked up by the wire services and reprinted in papers across the country, including one in Macon. Anjette read it and was crushed by Bob's betrayal of her. He'd been in love with her. He *told* her so. And now he was acting like they were little more than acquaintances.

On Wednesday afternoon, Anjette, surrounded by deputies, descended in the elevator to the courthouse basement for a probable cause hearing. Her wheelchair was rolled into Judge Earl Butler's outer office where she got to her feet with no assistance.

"I'm not going into that courtroom in a wheelchair. I'll walk on my own today," she told the deputies.

Her leg protested painfully, but walking unassisted that morning gave her a badly-needed feeling of control over something. She made her way slowly through a hallway and into the courtroom where she took her seat beside William Buffington and gave him her most winning smile.

Reporters and sightseers leaned forward for a look at the person fast becoming the best known woman in Georgia. Every detail of her appearance was reported in the papers. She was referred to as "the glamorous defendant". Her hair was alternately described as prematurely gray or platinum and the style—pageboy—was conscientiously noted. They watched every move she made.

Jetta and Alice Donovan sat close behind the defense table, but there was time only for a quick whispered greeting before the judge took the bench and the hearing began. Anjette sat absolutely still as he reduced the deaths of those four people to cold, precise legal language. Every eye in the room was on the defendant, but she showed no reaction at all.

Buffington immediately objected to having all four cases dealt with at once. "Mr. West should select one warrant and proceed under it before going on to the next."

"Your honor," West countered, "the evidence produced by the state will be admissible to each of the warrants involved. Any other presentation will make it necessary to present the same evidence four separate times."

Butler overruled the objection and the hearing continued.

The only witness called Wednesday was Dr. Larry Howard, who testified that he had examined tissue from all the victims and had found arsenic in all four samples. Although the defense raised questions as to the quantities of poison in each body, Howard couldn't be shaken on the single important fact: Ben Lyles, Buddy Gabbert, Julia Lyles and Marcia Lyles had all died of arsenic poisoning.

The hearing was adjourned at 5:00 P.M. and reconvened Thursday morning at 9:00. While the state presented a number of witnesses, the real stars of the day were two of Anjette's employees.

Carrie Jackson was the first on the witness stand. She gave Anjette a steady look, then with hands clasped tightly in her lap, gave her name.

"Where do you work, Carrie?" West asked.

"I'm a cook at Anjette's Restaurant."

"How long have you worked there?"

She stopped to think. "Twenty-six years."

"So you worked for the whole Lyles family?"

"Yes, sir."

He took her back to the time Julia Lyles was in the hospital. "All right, now, do you ever remember seeing Mrs. Anjette Lyles fix anything at the restaurant for Mrs. Ben Lyles, Sr.?"

"Yes, sir. I saw her fix—I fixed some chicken pie and she took some chicken pie and she took some buttermilk."

"Buttermilk?"

"Yes, sir."

"Now, how did you know that Mrs. Anjette Lyles was fixing that for Mrs. Ben Lyles?" he asked.

Carrie paused a moment, organizing her thoughts. "She told somebody to pour a half glass of buttermilk. Then she took the buttermilk and went out the back door and before she went out the back door, she got a little brown paper bag out of her overnight bag."

"All right," he said. "Then where did she go?"

"She went out the back door to go to the hospital where Mrs. Lyles was."

"Did you ever see her take anything out of that bag again?"

Carrie nodded. "Yes, sir, the next morning. On two mornings she did that."

West then asked similar questions about Anjette taking food or drink to the hospital when Marcia was a patient.

"I imagine it was about three or four days after she went in the hospital," Carrie told him. "One morning she squeezed two lemons in a glass and then she asked me if that was enough lemons. I asked her what she was going to do with it. She said she was going to make Marcia a lemonade. I told her, well, that should be enough."

"What did she do with it?"

"She set it up on top of the steam table and went out in the dining room. Done something out there. I don't know what she did."

"Then did she come back?" he asked.

Carrie nodded. "Yes, sir, she come back with her pocketbook. She took the pocketbook and the lemonade and went in the restroom with it."

"Then what did she do?"

"She came out and stirred it up and she told Carmen to come on, let's go to the hospital, 'cause she didn't want Marcia to die and she didn't see it and she wasn't there."

A whisper circulated through the courtroom, but stilled when Judge Butler looked up.

"She said what?" West asked.

"She told Carmen to come on and drive her up to the hospital, said she didn't want her child to die if she wasn't up there with her."

During a short recess, Anjette conversed with her mother and sister-in-law.

"How is Carla?"

"We don't know. We haven't talked to her."

"I wish I could see my little girl. She must be so scared."

Carmen Howard didn't want to be in that courtroom. She'd always gotten along with Anjette and didn't want to say anything that might harm her. However, her interviews with the deputies had left no doubt in her mind that she was expected to tell the court exactly what she'd told them. Under West's prompting, she described the scene in the restaurant kitchen much as Carrie Jackson had. Yes, she remembered

Anjette taking her pocketbook into the restroom with the glass of lemonade.

"Did you have occasion to see that pocketbook two weeks later?"

"Yes, sir. Mrs. Lyles asked me to change out her pocketbooks and I was taking everything out of the black one to put in another one."

"Did you find anything unusual in the black bag?"

She looked down, unhappy with the direction they were going. "Yes, sir. There was a brown paper bag. Inside was a bottle of ant poison."

This time the outburst in the courtroom required a couple of quick knocks with the gavel to quiet. Only Anjette remained silent and motionless.

"Was that the same brown bag the officers took with them the night they searched the house?"

"I think so."

West asked Carmen if she'd ever seen ant poison in the Pinewood house before and she told the court that they had been overrun with ants when they'd first moved in.

"We put the poison out in bottle caps then to kill the ants."

Next West asked her about the day of Marcia's funeral. Carmen testified that when she got to the Lyles house, she realized she had no gloves with her. She'd gone into Anjette's room to see if she could find a pair to borrow.

"Did you find any gloves?"

"No, sir."

"Did you find anything unusual?"

"Yes, sir," she said slowly. "There were two bottles of Ant Terro in one of her dresser drawers."

The court adjourned for lunch about noon.

Jetta leaned forward to ask her daughter, "What in the world is Carmen talking about? What's that about the ant poison?"

"It's all right, Mother. I just had it because we were having problems with ants at the restaurant."

The spectators filed out of the room and Jetta and Alice Donovan began moving down the center aisle. They'd almost reached the door to the corridor when Anjette called to Alice.

"Have them send me some chicken salad and french fries from the restaurant. Oh, and tell the person who has been putting sugar in my coffee to leave it out."

When the hearing resumed at one 1:00 P.M., Carmen returned to the stand and West asked her to describe what she found when she arrived at the Lyles home the Monday after Marcia's funeral.

"Mrs. Lyles was looking for something. She was pulling out all the old papers and pulling out boxes under the bed that had old papers in it. She said she was looking for a letter written by her mother-in-law. She tore out everything in the house and finally found the letter down in the lining in one of old Mrs. Lyles's pocketbooks."

"Is that Mrs. Ben Lyles, Sr., you mean?" West asked.

"Yes, sir, in her pocketbook."

"Did you read the letter yourself?"

"No, sir, but she told me something might come up and I was to say I found the letter."

Solicitor West then turned to the defense table and, in a loud voice, demanded that they produce this letter. "I understand that you have it in your safe."

Buffington's answer was short. "I'm not going to introduce any evidence for the benefit of the state."

Under cross examination, Buffington asked Carmen about Anjette's treatment of Carla and Marcia. "Did Mrs. Lyles take good care of her children?"

Carmen smiled. She was more comfortable with this kind of question. "Yes, sir."

"Did she appear to love them?"

"Yes, sir."

"And would you say she was a good mother?"

"Oh, yes, sir, I would," she said with conviction.

"In your five years working for the family, did you ever see Mrs. Lyles mistreat either of them?"

"No, sir, I never did."

William West's closing argument was brief, quickly reviewing the evidence that had been presented.

"There is no question but that each of the victims died of a lethal dose of arsenic poisoning and there is no question but that the defendant had in her possession a quantity of arsenic. There is certainly probable cause to have this case bound over to Superior Court."

Buffington argued the opposite during his closing. "The state does not have sufficient evidence to commit Anjette Lyles on these four murder charges. There is not even proof that three of these victims died of arsenic poisoning. We'll consent that the evidence showed that little Marcia died of poisoning, but there was no evidence that Mrs. Lyles administered the poison to the child."

He strenuously objected to the manner in which the tissue samples from the Veterans Hospital had been introduced. "Dr. Sikes admitted he couldn't definitely identify the bottle they were in. God knows that anyone who has ever been in the armed forces of the United States knows how inefficient the government is." That statement provoked appreciative laughter from the room. "And I assume that extends to the Veterans Administration. There's no proof that the organs from the VA Hospital examined by Dr. Howard were even Joe Neal Gabbert's organs.

"Your honor, the state is trying to snowball these four charges through this court on mere suspicion alone."

Earl Butler had listened without expression to both arguments. When they were through, he simply nodded and began writing his order there on the bench. The courtroom was silent until he finished and looked up. He delivered his decision in a clear, calm voice.

"It is strange to me that four persons of the same household died within six years and that arsenic is discovered in the organs of the four. In proceedings of this nature, the duty of this Court is simply to determine whether there is sufficient reason to suspect the guilt of the accused, and whenever such probable cause exists, it is the duty of this court to enter an order committing her.

"It is my opinion that it is my duty in view of the evidence to commit the defendant insofar as warrant number 36251-C, charging the defendant with the murder of Marcia Lyles, is concerned. And accordingly it is so ordered that she be committed to the Superior Court. I shall reserve the entry of any order in connection with the other three warrants until such time as the court reporter may be able to transcribe the record of the proceedings and I am able to review it."

William Buffington wasn't totally unhappy with the ruling.

"We did pretty good," Buffington quietly told his client as the courtroom emptied. "He could have committed on all four, but he only committed on one."

Anjette shook her head and tried to share his optimism, but it was difficult. She had hoped that the charges would be dismissed today and that she would be allowed to go home. It made no difference to her if she were committed on one or four charges. The result was the same — she would be returning to her jail cell.

"So the other cases are dismissed?" she asked, trying to sound hopeful.

"Well, no, not exactly. This was just the commitment hearing. If they want, they can present all of them to the Grand Jury for indictment. But let's just be glad that it went as well as it did today."

As Anjette passed another long night in the small cell, she found it hard to be glad about anything.

CHAPTER SEVEN

WILLIAM WEST WITHDREW AS PROSECUTOR IN THE MOST sensational case Macon had ever known because he was kin to the Lyles family. The relationship was a remote one. His wife's mother was Julia Lyles's mother-in-law's half sister, making him some degree of distant cousin, by marriage, to the murdered woman. There was no legal tenet that specifically prohibited his being involved, but West knew every aspect of this trial would be painstakingly examined and didn't want even a hint of impropriety. So he disqualified himself and his office from the prosecution.

When a case cannot be prosecuted locally, Georgia law provides for the appointment of a special prosecutor by the attorney general. So the matter of who would prosecute Anjette Lyles was turned over to the state. Of course it was still a local case, and William West's opinion in the matter carried considerable weight. He recommended a young lawyer whose work he trusted, Charles Adams. Adams had been hired as one of West's assistants when he was appointed Bibb County Solicitor General in 1952, and the young man did well under West's guidance. After gaining four years' experience prosecuting every kind of felony, Adams left the office and went into private practice with two other former prosecutors—Hank O'Neal and Bob Steele.

Charles Adams answered the telephone the morning William West called.

After pleasantries were exchanged, the Solicitor got to the point of his call—the Anjette Lyles murder case.

"You know I can't prosecute this case, don't you?"

"Yeah, I read in the paper you'd withdrawn," Adams said.

"Well, the attorney general's going to appoint a special prosecutor. Will you and Hank take the case? Will ya'll let him appoint you?"

Adams never hesitated. He almost ran into Hank's office to deliver the news. They were defense attorneys, true, but this was the chance of a lifetime. Prosecuting Anjette would generate tremendous publicity. The case might very well make them famous. And, on a more mundane level, they could use the money. Unlike what sometimes happened in private practice, they were sure to be paid for this one with their fee guaranteed by the county.

On June 2, Adams and O'Neal drove to Atlanta to meet with Attorney General Eugene Cook and Governor Marvin Griffin. When they started home later that day, their appointments were official. They were now the special prosecutors in the Anjette Lyles murder case.

"You know, I feel kind of strange about this," Adams said as they headed south along a two-lane highway. The sun had set and cool evening air blew in through the open windows. "I've always liked Anjette."

"Me, too. I always thought she was a real nice lady," Hank agreed. He tossed one spent cigarette out the window and lit another. "Wonder what made her do it?"

"I don't know. I can almost understand her killing her husbands, in a way. But killing that child doesn't make any damn sense at all."

The two men spent little time reflecting on Anjette's state of mind. The case was to be presented to the grand jury the next week and the few days remaining until then were spent in feverish activity — reviewing statements, discussing strategy and consulting with older attorneys for advice. The most pressing question was whether to include all the charges on a single indictment.

"If we do that," O'Neal pointed out, "we'll be sure to get all the evidence in, no matter which victim it relates to."

It was nearly midnight, and they would appear before the grand jury the next morning. They'd been over this same ground a hundred times, but they couldn't put the decision off any longer. Charles Adams's head ached with the effort of considering all the angles one last time. He'd drunk so much coffee that his stomach was in revolt and his eyes stung from the cigarette smoke hanging in his office.

"But if something goes wrong," Hank continued, "if we don't get a conviction, then she'll walk away. If we separate the charges, we'll have some insurance. Then if we don't get her on the first one, we can go back and get her on the next."

And that's what they decided. They spent the next hour preparing four separate indictments. Each was identical in form, accusing Anjette

Lyles of the offense of murder "by administering and causing to be administered deadly poisons" to the victims. The only differences were the names of the victims and the dates of the crimes.

At one-thirty, the two tired men left the Walnut Street building where their offices were located. They had time for only a few hours' sleep before they were due at the courthouse.

Tuesday morning was humid and hazy, promising temperatures in the 90s by afternoon. The grand jury convened at 9:00 A.M. and received the four proposed indictments. Twelve witnesses had been subpoenaed to testify in the closed proceeding and experienced court watchers predicted the session would last all day and on into the next.

The first witness was Dr. Leonard Campbell, who described for the jurors how the tissue samples from the four victims got to the state crime lab. He was followed by Dr. Larry Howard who explained the results of his tests on those tissue samples. Sheriff Wood and Chief Investigator John Gibson gave brief accounts of the execution of the search warrant and described what evidence had been seized. Carmen Howard and Carrie Jackson repeated essentially the same testimony they had given at the commitment hearing.

When Jackson was excused and left the grand jury room, Hank and Charles trailed out after her and had a quick word together in the corridor.

"Do you want to break for lunch now?" O'Neal asked.

Adams shook his head. "I don't think so. I think that does it."

"We've got six more witnesses," Hank objected.

"We don't need them." Charles was confident. "They've got more than enough to indict now. Why drag it out?"

Charles was right. The six had been enough. By twelve-thirty, the grand jury had finished its deliberations and four true bills were returned. Anjette had been indicted for all four murders.

Adams and O'Neal had known from the beginning that the case was going to be sensational, but they were unprepared for the depth of feeling it aroused in the community. It was rare that a day passed without a newspaper story about Anjette. No aspect of the case was too small to attract the attention of the press. Where two or more people gathered in Macon that summer, the Lyles case was the favorite topic of conversation. Memories stirred and the inevitable rumors sprang up about the possibility of other victims. How many other people had she poisoned? Any restaurant customer who had died within recent memory and whose symptoms could be stretched to fit arsenic poisoning was considered a likely victim. There were very few people straddling the fence on this subject, and the majority, their opinions unavoidably fashioned by the press coverage, believed Anjette was guilty.

Before becoming involved in the Lyles case, Charles and Hank had been able to walk the single block from their office to the courthouse in less than two minutes. Now the same trip could take up to half an hour. People stopped them at every turn to voice support or urge them on.

"You're doing a good job," a frail, elderly woman told Adams one morning. He belatedly recognized her as a friend of his mother's. "Now you just convict that woman!"

Even strangers called encouragement as they passed by.

The muggy days wore on, and the pending trial became their sole focus. When they weren't working on it, they were thinking about it. Their families complained they never saw them anymore. Workdays stretched well into the night, their office windows splashes of illumination in an otherwise sleeping town.

The case was expected to go to trial during the September term. Hank O'Neal and Charles Adams planned strategies, argued approaches and tried to anticipate everything that might happen at the trial. Witnesses were re-interviewed and facts were checked and double-checked. They debated the wisdom of trying all the charges at once and finally decided to try Anjette only for Marcia's murder.

"I think that's best," Adams said. "Marcia was the last one killed. The evidence is fresher. So are the witnesses. Besides, a lot of people can understand killing your husband or your mother-in-law, but killing a child ... that's something else."

They had method and financial motive, but some important questions had to be answered before they'd be confident enough to take the case to a jury. Neither Adams nor O'Neal had been involved with a poisoning case before, and they found it hard to understand how the deaths of four people could be caused by so common a product as a household insecticide.

"Ant poison is ant poison," Adams muttered. It was a hot June afternoon and the fans set up in the office offered little relief. "Who would think you could kill somebody with that stuff? I mean, you kill *insects* with it."

"Yeah," Hank agreed, "and how did all these killings go on without somebody noticing? They were all being treated by doctors, hell, they were in the *hospital* when they died. Somebody should have considered the possibility of poisoning long before Marcia's death."

They needed an expert, someone who could explain what had happened and was capable of presenting the facts in believable courtroom testimony. They found the man they needed nine hundred miles away.

Richard Ford was a nationally acknowledged authority on poisons. At the time Adams called him, he was the Medical Examiner for the city of Boston and Senior Pathologist for the Massachusetts State Police. Not only was he an expert in the field, Adams discovered, but Ford enjoyed sharing his considerable knowledge.

"That's simple," Ford said when asked how doctors could have failed to spot poisoning as the cause of death in the first three victims. "Doctors almost never arrive at a diagnosis of arsenic poisoning without some outside evidence to indicate it."

"What sort of evidence?"

"Well, it usually has to be something pretty direct—a patient suggesting he has been exposed to arsenic would probably do it or an empty container of the poison found in the area. Without that, the average physician would never make the correct diagnosis."

He also confirmed Dr. Howard's contention that the poison had been administered in small doses over a period of time.

"His findings would seem to support that. Besides, a large dose just wouldn't do it. That would simply cause nausea and vomiting and most of the poison would be expelled from the body."

Ford explained that arsenic attacked the weakest organs of the body, so that one patient might be thought to have died from heart trouble while in another the cause of death would appear to be a respiratory infection.

Adams was fascinated. He couldn't wait to share his new expertise with Hank. He'd heard of arsenic poisoning, of course, read about it in mystery novels and seen it in old movies, but he had never guessed how easy using it could be or how easily the cause of death could be overlooked. After only one phone call, he knew more about arsenic poisoning than he'd ever imagined existed. He knew they had to have Richard Ford testify for them.

June was a miserable month for Anjette. She hated where she was and how she looked. Except for court appearances, the only clothes she was allowed were cotton underwear and shapeless institutional dresses that made her surroundings even more drab than they'd first appeared. Sometimes her mother brought her food from the restaurant, but more often than not she was walked down the dim hallways to the inmate dining room and ate her bland meals there with the few other female prisoners in the jail. They were a rough group, loud and crude, and Anjette was a little afraid of them. She preferred the solitude of her cell.

Early in the month, she had sat helplessly in jail as the business she had poured so much time and money into was sold at auction to cover her outstanding debts and the attorneys' fees that were already beginning to pile up. Bill Lyles, Ben's uncle, had been the highest bidder. At least it was going to stay in the family. Foreclosure proceedings had also been initiated on the Pinewood Drive house. It was slated for auction the same day as the restaurant, but the sale was called off at the last minute when the attorney representing the bank that held the mortgage announced his clients felt sure their investment was secure. The fact that the house hadn't been sold brought Anjette little comfort. Even if she managed to get out of this mess, she'd never be able to pay what she owed on the house and her attorneys' bills were growing at an alarming rate.

She knew rumors about her continued to flourish. Jetta and Alice enjoyed sharing the latest gossip with her—most of the stories were so outrageous that they could all laugh about them. One tale making the rounds was that her jail cell was equipped with a luxurious mattress, air conditioning and a television. It wasn't true, of course. She had the same basic accommodations as any other prisoner—until late June. Then her circumstances changed for the worse.

A jail trustee was caught with money in an empty cigarette pack. It was a violation of the rules for any prisoner to have money and he knew it. When questioned, he told the jailers that Anjette had given it to him, along with instructions to buy her some Terro ant poison. This news caused near panic in the jail.

Sheriff Wood went to her cell and questioned her.

"That's crazy," she told him. "I didn't do that. Why would I?"

He had no idea what she'd intended to do it with the stuff. Acquiring the poison might have been the first step in an escape attempt. Or maybe she was overcome with remorse and wanted it to end her suffering. There was even a chance, one he thought of as remote, but possible, that the trustee had made up the story to avoid punishment for breaking the rules. Whatever the reason, Wood wasn't taking any chances with the most notorious prisoner he'd ever had.

He acted quickly, removing her from the general population in the women's section of the jail. They constructed a single cell especially for her, right under the courthouse dome. It was furnished with a cot, two metal stools and a toilet. One small, high window provided the only natural light — and a view of a brick air shaft. A rectangular opening in the metal door overlooked the main jail area and booking desk, so the sounds of the twenty-four hour jail operation drifted up to her, making a full night's sleep impossible. She heard the arrival of every angry criminal and every loud drunk, no matter what time of day they were arrested. Even when there were no arrests, her sleep was never sound. The courthouse clock, located in the tower above her head, struck every hour with deep, hollow strokes.

Anjette's new cell was the hottest place in the courthouse. When she complained, the matrons provided her with an oscillating electric fan that pushed the air around in a hot imitation of a breeze. Her meals were brought to her and the only exercise she got was the walk to and from the daily shower she was allowed.

Through the long summer of 1958, Anjette was held in isolation, allowed to see only her attorneys, her family and the jail officers. The only members of her family who set foot in the Bibb County Jail to see her were her mother and her sister-in-law, Alice Donovan.

CHAPTER EIGHT

THE BEST KEPT SECRET IN MACON THAT SUMMER WAS WHICH of the two Superior Court judges would preside over Anjette Lyles's murder trial. The judges themselves were determined to reserve that information until the last possible moment. When a pre-trial conference was held on August 12 to work out some of the logistics of conducting the biggest trial the town had ever seen, both Judge Oscar Long and Judge A. M. Anderson met with the prosecutors and defense attorneys. They weren't giving anything away.

The most pressing question was the date of the trial itself. It was originally to have been included in the September term, but as the end of summer approached, it became clear that conducting this trial, with its numerous witnesses and record number of prospective jurors, on a calendar with other cases would be an impossible task. So a special session was set for the Lyles case alone beginning October 6.

The defense team had spent hundreds of hours preparing for the case. William Buffington had flown thousands of miles that summer, learning what he could about the victims and interviewing those witnesses who would talk with him.

Charles Adams had felt for months that they were missing an important piece of evidence.

"I'm not comfortable with Gabbert's tissue samples," he told O'Neal. "You remember all the problems West had with that during the commitment hearing."

"Yeah." O'Neal laughed. "What was it Buffington said? 'Everyone knows how inefficient the government is. I assume the Veterans Administration is, too.' And I didn't much like Sikes's testimony. It's a weak spot. You're right."

They decided to strengthen it. Declaring that the samples taken after his death weren't sufficient for all the procedures necessary, the prosecution announced that Dr. Herman Jones, Director of the Georgia

State Crime Lab, would travel to Texas to exhume Buddy Gabbert's body and to obtain additional samples for testing. Jones and Larry Howard boarded a plane at Atlanta Airport early on the morning of August 28. It was mid-afternoon when they landed at El Paso, Texas. They stepped off the plane into heat that made the Atlanta summer seem mild by comparison, and were driven from the airport directly to the cemetery.

There they stood in the scorching sun as the mortuary workers dug into the grave. Standing beside them were two solemn-faced men—Buddy Gabbert's father and brother. They didn't speak as the dirt was removed from the grave. When the casket was finally raised from the ground and opened, both men stepped forward and looked inside.

"That's him," his father said quiet, sad voice. "That's Buddy."

"Yes, it's him," his brother agreed.

Although some deterioration had occurred, neither man had any difficulty in identifying the body. And any doubt would have been erased by the sight of two small items in the casket.

"That's the little Bible my mother put in the casket with him," D. K. Gabbert said. "And the little model airplane."

Both items were just where they'd been placed.

"You folks might be more comfortable over there under those trees," Dr. Jones told them before beginning his work. He waited until the Gabberts were on the other side of the cemetery before he made his first incision. The pathologists worked quickly, taking photographs and removing and storing samples. Then the casket was closed again. Howard and Jones returned to Atlanta that same day.

In her cell, Anjette read about the doctors' trip west and its gruesome purpose. She was allowed a subscription to one of the local papers and read it every day from front to back. She had asked for a radio, but the request had been refused, so she read, although it was not an activity she particularly enjoyed. It was much too lonely a pastime for her taste. Along with the newspapers she was given bound volumes of Reader's Digest condensed books. There was little else to do except anticipate the weekly visits from her mother or pass the time of day with her jailers and drink Coca-Colas. She was unusually fond of the soft drink, and they gave her several bottles every day.

Ollie Goings had been with the Bibb County Sheriff's Office for a number of years, and was working as a patrol officer when Anjette was arrested. A month or so later, he accepted the job of Chief Jailer because, as he always said later, nobody else would take it. Being Chief Jailer wasn't just a simple matter of stepping into a vacant position. Ollie might have had the title, but the decision involved his whole family. As was common practice at the time, the Chief Jailer was expected to live on the premises. He moved his wife Byrice and several of their eight children into the seven-room apartment on the fifth floor of the courthouse that was provided for the Chief Jailer. Their youngest child, Debbie, was still a toddler when they moved in. The county provided them with a maid to look after the apartment and do the cooking for the family. Byrice, in turn, supervised the jail's kitchen where the female inmates cooked the meals for all the prisoners.

In September, Judge Oscar Long sent word for Ollie to come to his chambers. The jailer arrived a few minutes later.

"Yes, sir. What can I do for you?"

The judge leaned back in his chair and frowned. "How is Anjette Lyles doing?"

"She seems okay."

"Well, I'm a little worried about her. You know, the trial's been scheduled for October and there's been some talk she might try to commit suicide."

"I sure haven't seen anything that would make me think that," Ollie said.

But Long didn't want to take any risks. "I'd still feel better if we had someone sitting with her, at least during the day."

So Ollie arranged the suicide watch. At night, the matron, Mrs. Stripling, made regular checks on their famous prisoner. The daytime duty fell to his wife, Byrice.

When the reason for the supervision was explained to Anjette, she laughed out loud.

"If I don't die till I kill myself," she told Byrice, "I'll be sitting right here till Gabriel blows his horn."

Byrice initially had been nervous when she entered the cell, but after only a few minutes, she began to feel at ease with Anjette. The prisoner was delighted to have the company.

"They don't know it, but they're doing me a favor. It's hell in this cell by myself. I'm glad to have you."

The two women had been acquainted for several years. Byrice and her daughter, Virginia, had been regular lunch customers at Anjette's Restaurant. But the two had never had more than a casual conversation. Now they had plenty of time to talk. In fact, there was nothing else to do. Byrice sat with Anjette in her cell twelve hours a day, and the two talked for hours on end.

Anjette had been all over the country and Byrice was eager to hear about her travels. They discussed clothes and current events, old times and mutual acquaintances. A friendship began to develop. Byrice made Anjette's world brighter and warmer and gave her something to look forward to again. Byrice often had lunch for them brought to the cell — not the dreary jailhouse food, but lunch prepared by her own maid. And the best part was that Byrice actually believed her to be innocent.

"I loved my child," Anjette told her more than once. "I didn't love her daddy, but I loved her. You know, if I'd wanted to kill her, I could have done it in such a way nobody would have known. You know, once she had meningitis. I could have said I didn't realize she was that sick and just let her die. But I didn't. As soon as I saw how sick she was, I rushed her to the hospital."

Byrice believed her and Anjette was pathetically grateful for that. For the first time in months, when she declared her innocence someone looked at her with trust instead of doubt. The belief of just one other human being was a wonderful thing.

Ollie Goings, however, didn't share his wife's assessment.

"I don't believe she killed that child," Byrice told him after dinner one night. They were sitting on their terrace that overlooked downtown Macon. "She just couldn't have done it."

"You're too soft-hearted," Ollie told her.

"No, I know she didn't. She really *talks* to me. I'd know if she'd killed those people."

Anjette became very fond of Byrice. In her, she found the acceptance and love she'd never had from her own mother. Jetta still came to see her once a week, but the visits weren't always pleasant. Too often they were stormy encounters that deteriorated into screaming matches between mother and daughter. Byrice started sitting in the room during these visits to try and keep the peace. While Anjette could be kept calm, Jetta often lost control. When Byrice asked Anjette about her mother's behavior, Anjette was philosophical.

"That's just the way she is. She's always been like that."

"I can't understand how she can be so hateful to her own daughter," Byrice told her husband.

He shook his head. "That Jetta's the meanest woman—always cursing and screaming. She'll holler at anybody."

Her behavior got so bad in September that Ollie barred her from the jail for a week.

Byrice Goings often found herself in sympathy with the female prisoners. She'd occasionally allow one of them to visit in her apartment to give them a break from the cell block and Anjette was no exception. In fact, she and Byrice got along so well that, on many days, the "suicide watch" took place in Byrice's living room.

One afternoon Anjette complained about her hair, which had now grown below her shoulders.

"It's driving me crazy. It's so hot!"

Byrice gave a little smile. "We could cut it."

"Really? You know how to cut hair?"

"Sure. I've cut the children's hair for years. Come on. Let's do it. It'll be cute."

An hour later, Anjette was sporting a new hairdo. It was much shorter and fluffed out around her head. The absence of all that thick hair gave her a cool, light-headed feeling. She loved it.

Debbie Goings grew so fond of Anjette that she often begged her mother to let her come for a visit. "I want my Jette. I want my Jette," the little girl would cry.

When Anjette was in the apartment, Byrice often let Debbie go out onto the terrace with the prisoner. Anjette would sit on the floor for hours, playing with the child. One early autumn afternoon, Byrice's daughter-in-law stopped by for a visit. She stood in the apartment and watched Anjette and Debbie on the terrace. Anjette was drinking a Coca-Cola—her favorite refreshment—and Debbie asked for a sip. Anjette handed her the bottle. The child put it to her lips, drank and gave it back. Byrice's daughter-in-law was horrified.

"How can you let her drink from that woman's bottle?" she asked, not bothering to keep her voice down. "It's dangerous."

Byrice wasn't bothered. "Why, the poor woman's been locked up for months. She can't hurt anyone. Besides, she's as sweet as she can be."

Preparations for the trial continued. With over fifty witnesses under subpoena and four hundred jurors expected to respond to notices, the judges knew that managing the trial was sure to present some unique problems. On September 29, Judges Long and Anderson held a meeting with representatives of the media and asked for recommendations.

A newspaper reporter made the first suggestion. "We'd like to take photographs during the trial. The public is very interested in this case and they have a right to see what is going on."

Judge Anderson didn't agree. "I know the Constitution guarantees a public trial, but doing what you want would be the same as forcing the defendant to stand trial in an arena." Photographs during the trial would not be allowed.

A woman from a local radio station spoke next. "Can part of the courtroom be set aside for reporters? With all the interest in the trial, the press will have to fight to find a place to sit."

The judges saw this as a reasonable request, and agreed to reserve a section of the balcony for them.

"But that's not going to be enough seats," the woman objected.

It was decided that each news medium would be assigned two seats and issued passes. The reporters had to be happy with that. The judges also declared that they weren't going to have people running in and out of the courtroom all day.

"People will be admitted only during the recesses," Judge Long said. "And once all the seats are filled, the doors will be closed. I want the Sheriff's Department to rope off the area around the main doors to keep people from milling around the entrance while court's in session."

Ollie Goings was also dealing with the press, but he didn't have the same authority as the judges. There were no orders he could give to keep them away from his jail. He had to cope with the reporters on a daily basis. A cluster of them were always waiting at the courthouse doors, ready to pounce on anyone even distantly connected to the case. Worse than that, they tried to sneak into the jail at all hours. The photographers were the biggest pests. They were desperate for a picture of Anjette in her cell. Every time the telephone rang, there was a better than even chance it was a reporter. They even called the Chief Jailer at home.

One night around 2:00 A.M., the telephone rang. Goings got out of bed and made his way to the hall where he answered it. Less than a minute later, he slammed the receiver down.

Byrice was sitting up in the bed, alarmed by the late call. "What was it?"

"Another reporter! From London, England! Calling at this time of night! I swear, all it is around here is eat, sleep and breathe Anjette Lyles and I'm sick of it!"

Byrice had her share of encounters with the press as well. They'd call her and pretend to be an old acquaintance or tell her they were taking a survey, then start asking questions about Anjette. By the end of September, she was almost afraid to answer her own telephone.

October arrived unseasonably warm, as if summer didn't want to let go just yet. Several days before the trial, reporters from the Atlanta papers and the wire services began arriving in town. Celestine Sibley was assigned to cover the case for the *Atlanta Constitution*. She was a natural for the job, having a number of murder trials already under her belt and having recently published a mystery novel. Her colleagues jokingly referred to her as the Murder Queen.

The horde of reporters scoured the countryside, looking for stories. They visited the churchyards where the victims were buried and interviewed any of the witnesses who would talk to them. Celestine and her photographer, Bill Wilson, even found one of Anjette's fortune tellers and interviewed him.

There had been some speculation that the defense would ask for a change of venue due to the excessive pre-trial publicity, but Buffington told Anjette that wasn't going to happen.

"People know you here, they like you. Our chances are just as good in Macon as they are anywhere else."

The next morning, he issued a statement that they would not request a change of venue.

"We are confident," it read in part, "that the good people of Bibb County will not have had their minds swayed by what they have read or heard, and will consequently afford her the fair trial to which she is entitled under the laws of the sovereign state of Georgia. I wish to state openly to the public that we shall enter a plea of 'not guilty'. In this connection, this is the only plea that could conceivably be entered because we want to stress again that Mrs. Lyles's only comment with regard to these charges is that she has committed no crime."

The first day of the trial was hot, hazy and sultry. Tropical storm Janice was roiling around the Caribbean, pounding south Florida with heavy rain and high winds. The drenching rain had not extended as far north as Macon, but the humid air settling over the town owed its oppressiveness to the southern storm.

Anjette was awake long before sunrise. This was the day she'd been waiting for, the chance to clear her name. She paced the confines of her cell, eager for the proceedings to start.

After breakfast, she dressed in a plain black dress her mother had brought for the occasion. She'd gained weight during her sedentary days behind bars, and the dress was two sizes larger than she'd been accustomed to wearing. At her waist, she fastened a belt with a rhinestone buckle. She applied her make up with a steady hand, gazing without expression into the mirror. Her newly-shortened hair feathered back attractively from her face.

Early the same morning, prospective juror Robert MacGregor knotted his necktie and spoke to his wife. "I know I won't be picked. You work for Dr. Ireland and he's going to be a witness. You know they won't let me be on that jury."

Edwin Connally, another Macon resident who'd been summoned to jury duty, was equally sure he would be turned down.

"You can drive me to the courthouse this morning and keep the car," he told his wife over breakfast. "Then come back and pick me up about five o'clock. They won't choose me. I know all the lawyers, and I used to eat lunch at Anjette's every day.

But knowing Anjette Lyles wasn't uncommon for anyone in Macon. She had grown up in the town, and her restaurant had been a popular eating place for years. She knew all the principal players in the case and had at least a nodding acquaintance with a number of people in the jury pool.

At 8:55 A.M., Anjette strode into the second-floor courtroom with a deputy beside her. She carried a white Bible. Anjette's appearance caused a ripple of talk in the big, high-ceilinged room. She hadn't been seen in public since the commitment hearing and her appearance had changed. Reporters quickly scribbled the details of her dress, her new haircut, even the earrings she wore. And the fact that she'd gained weight was noted with considerable relish. But she was still a remarkably attractive woman.

She took her place at the defense table with her three attorneys. Jetta Donovan, Alice Donovan and Anjette's uncle, Lewis Watkins, joined the semi-circle of chairs at the table. The deputy sat directly behind the prisoner. A few feet away at the prosecution table, O'Neal and Adams opened their briefcases and spread papers across the wooden surface. Sitting quietly beside them was Harry Harris, the lead investigator on the case.

At exactly 9:00 A.M., the door behind the bench opened and the question of which judge would preside over the case was answered. Judge Oscar Long took his place and called the session to order. A widely respected man, he was considered intelligent and fair by both sides. He was 55 years old and had been on the bench since his election to the judgeship in 1954.

Hank O'Neal rose to his feet. He was an attractive young man who sported a crewcut that gave him the appearance of a college boy rather than the experienced trial attorney that he was. In a strong, clear voice he read the indictment that formally charged Anjette with the murder of her daughter.

William Buffington entered the official plea of "not guilty" and the first panel of forty-eight jurors was brought into the courtroom.

O'Neal swore in the panel and handled the prosecution's initial questions, including the expected ones about being related to the defendant and having preconceived ideas about her guilt. Twenty people were disqualified in that phase.

Anjette put her head close to William Buffington's. "How can that many people think I'm *guilty*?"

"Shhhh. We'll talk about it later."

He got to his feet. It was the defense's turn to ask questions. Buffington covered a lot of ground with the remaining jurors— employment, church, family, feelings about women and any connection they might have had with the case or anyone involved. Mere acquaintance with the defendant or some other party wasn't sufficient for disqualification. In a small town like Macon, it would have been nearly impossible to find twelve jurors who had never met any of the parties to the case.

Charles Adams then stood and asked each juror one question. "If you were convinced of the guilt of this defendant, would you impose the death sentence on her as readily as you would on a man?"

When Edwin Connally was asked that question, he said, "Yes, sir. I'm a Christian and I believe in capital punishment."

Connally, who'd been so sure he wouldn't be chosen, was the first juror selected.

Anjette watched as each prospective juror was questioned. Buffington had given her a copy of the jury list, and from time to time she glanced at the names. Once or twice, she leaned over to her mother and whispered a comment about one of the prospective jurors.

"Isn't that the man who used to work with Daddy?" she asked once, pointing to Barney Upton.

"Yes. He was with the railroad when your father was."

As the day progressed, the jury box began to fill. Robert MacGregor was chosen in spite of his wife's association with Dr. Ireland, as was Barney Upton, who at 62 was the oldest juror.

Most of the time, Anjette sat with her hands resting in her lap, calmly watching the proceedings around her. She glanced at the jurors as they filed into the box, but only once did she seem to make contact with any of them. When one of her attorneys gave the town of Vienna the European rather than the Georgian pronunciation, she shared a quick smile with some of the men.

By 5:00 P.M., ten jurors—all men—had been selected. In addition to MacGregor, Upton and Connally, there were seven others in the jury box: Edward Wheeler, Collis Roach, John Neal, Paul Lucas, H. D. Murrell, Charles Bartlett and Chester Stevenson. Judge Long ordered the partial jury be sequestered and adjourned the proceedings until Tuesday morning.

The county was spared the expense of housing the jurors in a hotel because there was space for them in the courthouse. They were put in a dormitory room on the top floor—the same floor as the jail. It was furnished with fourteen single beds and there was a shower room just down the hall.

"If you need anything," the bailiffs told them, "give us a list and we'll call your wives."

It had been an exhausting day for the defendant. In order to reach the elevator that would take her back to the fifth floor, she had to cross a public corridor. That afternoon it was jammed with reporters and photographers. As she made her way across the hall, accompanied by deputies and her mother and sister-in-law, they surged forward, calling her name, popping flashbulbs in her face and shouting questions. Anjette stood stoically in the midst of the chaos, ignoring them. But Jetta Donovan hated the crush and tried to cover her face to avoid the cameras. This did nothing to discourage them. The reporters just shouted all the louder and the photographers knelt near the floor, aiming their cameras upward, trying to get a better view of her. Jetta finally lost control.

"Damn you," she snapped at them, swinging her purse in the direction of their faces until they were forced to move back. When the elevator doors finally opened, she fell back inside the car and glared at them as the doors closed.

1. Anjette Donovan Lyles, ca. 1950 — courtesy of *The Macon Telegraph*

2. Ben F. Lyles, Jr., ca. 1950 — courtesy of The *Macon Telegraph*

3. Anjette Lyles with daughters Marcia and Carla, 4/24/58 —
courtesy of *The Macon Telegraph*

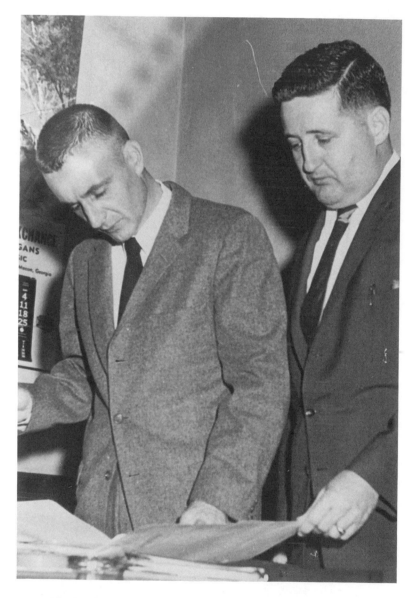

4. Hank O'Neal and Charles Adams, 1958 — courtesy of
The Macon Telegraph

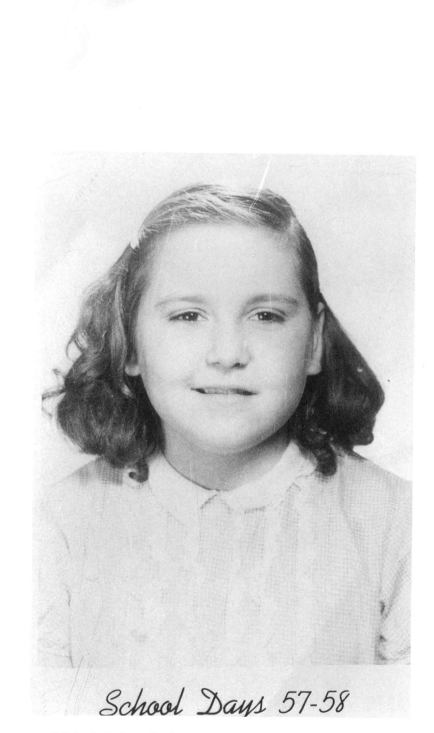

School Days 57-58

5. Marcia Lyles, school picture 1957-1958 school year —
   courtesy of *The Macon Telegraph*

6. Jack Gautier, 10/19/56 — courtesy of *The Macon Telegraph*

7. J. Taylor Phillips, 5/21/52 — courtesy of *The Macon Telegraph*

8. Roy Rhodenhiser, 1/30/51 — courtesy of *The Macon Telegraph*

9. Julia Young Lyles — courtesy of *The Macon Telegraph*

10. Lester Chapman, 2/21/58 — courtesy of *The Macon Telegraph*

11. Candles, roots and powders seized from Anjette Lyles's home — courtesy of *The Macon Telegraph*

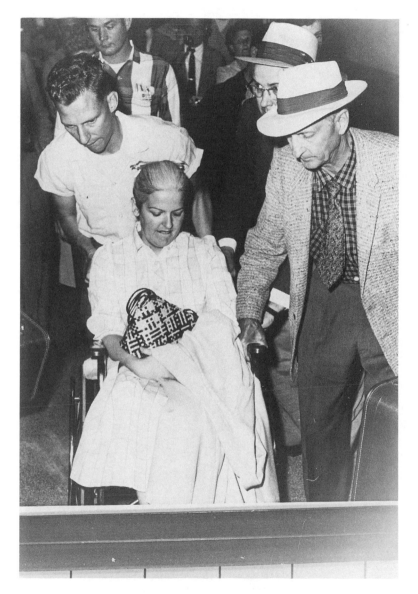

12. Anjette Lyles being transferred from Macon Hospital to the
    Bibb County Jail, 5/7/58 — courtesy of *The Macon Telegraph*

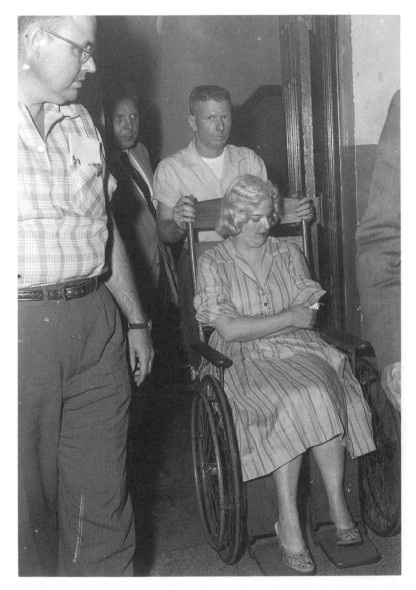

13. Anjette Lyles at her commitment hearing, 5/15/58 — courtesy of *The Macon Telegraph*

14. Anjette Lyles entering the courtroom at her commitment hearing, 5/15/58 — courtesy of *The Macon Telegraph*

15. Crowd in Bibb County Courthouse for Lyles murder trial, October, 1958 — courtesy of *The Macon Telegraph*

16. Anjette Lyles entering courtroom, October, 1958 —
courtesy of *The Macon Telegraph*

17. Anjette Lyles in the courtroom, October, 1958 — courtesy of *The Macon Telegraph*

18. Anjette Lyles and Latrelle West entering Sheriff Wood's car for trip to Reidsville Prison, 8/4/59 — courtesy of *The Macon Telegraph*

19. Anjette Lyles leaving Bibb County Courthouse for Reidsville State Prison, 8/4/59 — courtesy of *The Macon Telegraph*

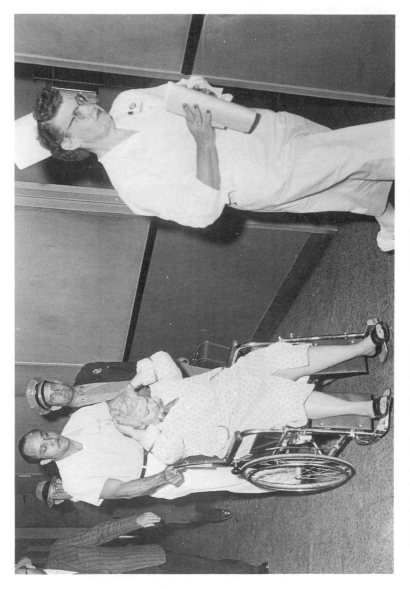

20. Anjette Lyles in hospital, 2/24/59 — courtesy of *The Macon Telegraph*

21. Watkins/Donovan/Lyles family burial plot, Coleman's Chapel cemetery, Wadley, Georgia — photo by Jaclyn White

22. Anjette Lyles's headstone, Coleman's Chapel cemetery — photo by Jaclyn White

CHAPTER NINE

TUESDAY MORNING THEY WENT BACK TO COURT. JURY SELEC-
tion was complete by 11:00 A.M., sooner than anyone had predicted.
William Newberry and Mark Carraway completed the jury panel, and
Mackey Clark and Frank Comer were chosen as alternates. One reason
the process went so quickly was that the prosecution hadn't spent an
excessive amount of time questioning prospective jurors. They had no
ideal juror in mind. All they wanted were everyday people.

"A mother killing a child," Adams had said during one of their late-
night strategy sessions. "If we can prove she killed that child, *any* jury
will convict her. Why waste time looking for a certain kind of juror?"

On this second day of the trial, the courtroom was filled to capacity,
and a large crowd stood in the corridors waiting for others to leave so
that they might take their vacated seats. The mostly female audience
packed onto the wooden benches was in a state of high excitement. This
was as close to real drama as most of them would ever be. Anjette could
feel their eyes on her, watching everything she did.

O'Neal and Adams knew each other well. They'd worked together a
long time and were comfortable with one another's strengths. It was
generally accepted that Hank's greatest talent lay in guiding witnesses
through their testimony and in cross-examination. Charles's strength
was his ability to address jurors. Opening statements and closing
arguments were his specialties. Just before noon, he stood before the
new jury. He was a smiling man with bright blue eyes, immediately
likable. His friendly manner made his words seem casual, almost
unplanned, but he had earned a reputation for being very thorough.
He never overlooked an important element and knew instinctively
which points needed emphasis.

Anjette watched Adams, never letting any expression cross her face,
as he outlined the state's case against her.

"Anjette Lyles is one of the most scheming women that anyone could imagine. She killed four people who loved her out of hate and out of greed. As the case is presented to you in this courtroom, you are going to hear a chilling tale of malice and greed."

He began his story with her first marriage, telling them that Ben Lyles hadn't been ambitious enough for his wife. "He died practically insane with arsenic. And his death brought Anjette $1,200."

He painted a pathetic picture of Joe Neal Gabbert and his declining health. "This young man was reduced from a six footer, a two hundred pounder, to a cold corpse."

One row behind Anjette sat Mr. and Mrs. Turner Neal, Buddy's aunt and uncle. They had flown to Macon from their Arkansas farm at the request of Gabbert's parents, who were too ill to travel. When Adams described their nephew's death, Mrs. Neal cried softly and dabbed at her eyes with a handkerchief.

"She profited from that death, too," Adams continued, "this time in the amount of $20,000. But she was broke ninety days later. Anjette Lyles spent money like a drunken sailor."

William Buffington jumped to his feet at that statement, objecting violently.

Judge Long looked to Adams for his answer.

"I think we'll be able to prove it, your honor."

"Overruled."

Adams went on to describe Julia's death and Marcia's suffering. "As Marcia Lyles screamed in terror from hallucinations caused by the poisoning, the defendant laughed at her."

For once, Anjette's reserve slipped. She closed her eyes and pressed her lips together in a tight line. Spectators watched for more reaction, but her face grew calm and expressionless once more.

Adams was relentless. "Gentlemen, the state will prove that Anjette Lyles fed deadly poisons to her victims even while she sat by their bedsides, supposedly nursing them. These crimes are so vile, so premeditated, so brutal that if we prove them to your satisfaction, there can be only one verdict. And we will ask the death penalty."

After the lunch recess, defense attorney Jack Gautier moved to exclude all mention of the other indictments pending against his client.

"Your honor, it puts the defendant in the position of having to defend more than one case at a time and prejudices the other three cases which are pending."

O'Neal countered with a Georgia Supreme Court decision that permitted any evidence to be admitted when a defendant is on trial for a series of crimes. After some heated back-and-forth discussion, Judge Long denied Gautier's motion. O'Neal and Adams had won a major battle before they had even presented their first witness.

Hank O'Neal's immediate task was to introduce the jury to the victims and to prove that the bodies which had been autopsied—and in which arsenic was found—were indeed those of Ben Lyles, Julia Lyles, Joe Neal Gabbert and Marcia Lyles.

He called Hoke Smith, the local mortician who had embalmed Buddy, Julia and Marcia, as his first witness. Anticipating a defense tactic, the prosecutor spent some time establishing the type of embalming fluid that had been used.

"Now do you recall the specific type of embalming fluid used on Joe Neal Gabbert?"

"Yes, I do. It was a fluid manufactured by the Champion Chemical Company, goes under the trade name of Champion Specialist."

"What fluid, if any, was used on Mrs. Julia Young Lyles?"

"A fluid manufactured by the Hydrol Chemical Company," Smith said. "It goes under the trade name of Velva-Glo."

"And what was used on the child, Marcia Elaine Lyles?"

"It was the same brand, Velva-Glo," Smith said, adding that he had provided a sample of Velva-Glo to Medical Examiner Leonard Campbell.

William Buffington was a tall, thin, serious man. He didn't smile when he began his cross examination. This was serious business and he wanted everyone to know it.

"Now, Mr. Smith, do you know the component parts of this embalming fluid you used on Marcia yourself?"

"I know the making ingredients. Other than that, I have no idea as to how it is mixed or the chemical analysis of it—except what is on the label."

Buffington pursued that thought. "Well, sir, if you don't know beyond what you see on the label, then you don't really know whether there was any arsenic in there or not, do you?"

"Yes, sir. There's one little notation on the label, says the state laws prohibit the use of any poisonous materials in this liquid. And I believe it is controlled by the Pure Food and Drug Act."

Buffington asked several more questions about the fluids used on Gabbert and Mrs. Lyles, but made no progress. Before releasing Smith from the witness stand, he tried one last time.

"Now, it is true, is it not, Mr. Smith, that arsenic or arsenic compounds were used rather generally in embalming fluids up until fairly recently?" When Smith did not agree immediately, Buffington went on. "I will define 'recently' then. How recently, Mr. Smith, did you cease to use embalming fluid that contained arsenic?"

"I have never used it in the practice of my profession in the past twenty-two years, sir."

"But it has been used in your profession, has it not?"

"Yes, sir, some years ago."

"You know whether or not that it would have been used back as recently as 1950?"

"No, sir."

"You just don't know whether it was or not."

Smith was growing irritable at the repeated questions. "It wouldn't have been used in 1950, no sir, because the Pure Food and Drug Act stopped it back years ago."

A. R. King made a brief appearance to testify that he had been present when Ben Lyles and Julia Lyles were buried and when Gabbert's body was disinterred for removal to Texas. He also told the court he had moved Ben Lyles's body from Cochran to Wadley, at Anjette's request.

The afternoon passed slowly. The temperature in the stuffy courtroom rose as the day advanced in spite of the air conditioning that was supposed to keep it cool. The warmth of the room combined with the dry testimony caused a number of the spectators' heads to nod.

But Anjette's attention didn't wander, even for a moment. She jotted down ideas during the testimony and occasionally passed notes to Buffington, suggesting questions he might ask. Alert as she was, the long hours still took a toll on her. Every now and then, as unobtrusively as she could, she repositioned herself in the hard wooden chair and straightened to her full seated height, trying to ease the tension in her back and neck.

The prosecution next called David Banks. The young police officer looked tired—and with good reason. His first child had been born during the night and he'd had no sleep. Banks raised his hand and swore to tell the truth.

Yes, he testified, he had known both Ben Lyles, Jr. and his mother, Julia Lyles.

"Now," O'Neal asked, "were you present at the time Ben Lyles, Jr. was disinterred for the purpose of an autopsy?"

Banks coughed nervously. "Yes, sir."

"And what was the purpose of your going?"

"To identify the body."

"All right, sir. Now, were you present down there in the cemetery when Mrs. Ben Lyles, Sr. was disinterred?'

Banks paused a few seconds as if remembering the scene. "Yes, sir."

"Did you see the grave of Mrs. Ben Lyles, Sr., opened?"

Banks shifted in his chair, uneasy with the memory. "Yes, sir."

"Did you see the lady who was in the casket there?"

"Yes, sir."

"Who was that individual?"

"Mrs. Ben Lyles, Sr."

"And that is the lady that was autopsied?" O'Neal asked.

"Yes, sir."

O'Neal continued. "All right, sir. Now did you see the grave of Mr. Ben Lyles, Jr., opened?"

"Yes, sir."

"Did you see the occupant of that grave?"

"Yes."

"Had some portions of his face or neck deteriorated to any extent?"

Banks swallowed hard. "Yes, sir. Down in the neck ... the lower part of the chin and upper part of the neck ..." He put a hand on his own throat. "Right here. From his ... " He cleared his throat again and started over. "The profile from his nose up was all right."

"Did you recognize that man as being Ben F. Lyles, Jr.?"

Banks nodded. "Yes, sir."

"By the way, was he autopsied there, Mr. Banks?"

"Yes, sir."

"Did anything happen to you at the time of the autopsy?"

"Yes, sir. I ... I had to leave. It was too much for my stomach."

"You get sick?" O'Neal asked

"Yes, sir."

After only a mild attempt to challenge Banks's identification of Ben and Julia, Buffington allowed the sleepy officer to leave the stand. The man's discomfort had been so apparent that everyone in the courtroom, including the defense attorneys, was glad his testimony was over.

Despite Judge Long's earlier ruling, Jack Gautier continued to object every time a death other than Marcia's was mentioned. The judge patiently overruled each objection, but the constant interruptions slowed the trial.

Shortly before 3:00 P.M., Judge Long called for a fifteen minute recess. Anjette didn't leave the courtroom, but took advantage of the break to walk around the immediate area.

When court reconvened, D. K. Gabbert took the stand. Buddy's brother was a big, soft-spoken man. A furniture salesman in El Paso, Texas, he had never enjoyed being the center of attention. He treated the presentation of his testimony as an unpleasant duty to be done as well and as quickly as possible. O'Neal put him through the paces.

"At the time of your brother's death, Mr. Gabbert, how old was he?"

"Twenty-six."

"Now, I'll ask you to give a brief physical description of your brother."

"My brother was over six feet tall, very rugged and in good health."

"Have you ever known him to have any serious maladies of any kind?"

"Not to my knowledge."

O'Neal consulted a notepad at the prosecution table, then asked, "When your brother died, how did you first find it out?"

"Through a telephone call from Anjette Lyles Gabbert." He looked at the defense table where he briefly met Anjette's steady gaze.

"Where were you when you received it?"

"El Paso, Texas."

O'Neal moved on to the day of Buddy's funeral.

"On that occasion that you were here for that funeral, on the day of the funeral, did you attend a supper anywhere?"

"Yes. At Anjette Lyles's house.

"Had you known her before that time?"

"No."

O'Neal glanced meaningfully at the defendant. "Did you have an opportunity on the day of that funeral while you were attending this supper that you've just mentioned to observe her demeanor?"

"Yes, I did."

"Was it one of grief or sorrow, or what was it?"

Gabbert's jaw tightened in anger. "No, it was one more of levity. I didn't notice any particular sorrow or grief."

O'Neal paused a minute to let that sink in, then led him through a description of the burial after Buddy's body was returned to Texas in June of 1957. "Now, Mr. Gabbert, listen to these lines which I quote to you and I shall ask you some questions. 'Let not your heart be troubled. Ye believe in God, believe also in me. In my Father's house are many mansions.' I ask you, have you ever heard those lines before?"

"I recognize that as the scripture from the fourteenth chapter of John."

Anjette glanced down at the Bible in her lap, then back at the witness.

"At the time of the burial of your brother in Texas, was any use made of those particular passages of scripture?"

Gabbert's eyes filled and he had to swallow hard before answering. "My mother wrote them in a little white Bible at the time he was buried in Texas and put it in the casket with him. She also slipped a little model plane in, too."

O'Neal asked if the witness had been present when Buddy's body was exhumed for autopsy. D. K. said he had been.

"Did you find anything in connection with those lines at the time your brother was exhumed?"

"The Bible was open to the fourteenth chapter of John."

"Just as it had been placed in there when he was buried?"

"Correct."

"And the little plane?"

"It was there, too."

Several spectators dabbed their eyes as Gabbert left the stand.

Leonard Campbell was the last witness of the day. He took the stand in a matter-of-fact manner and recounted how he'd performed a post-mortem examination on Marcia at Parkview Hospital the night she died, how he'd removed some small amounts of tissue from her body and later examined them under a microscope. He believed at that time, he said, that she had died due to some rare organism in the lung. However, a few hours later he was contacted by Bibb County Coroner Lester Chapman, who gave him some new information.

This reference to new information was frustrating to the spectators since the doctor didn't elaborate further. Hank O'Neal, conscious of the prohibitions on hearsay, didn't ask for an explanation.

"As a result of that information, did you have occasion to see Marcia Lyles again?"

"I did, at the funeral home, Memorial Chapel."

He described how he had removed additional tissue samples from her body on April 6 and sent them to the Georgia State Crime Laboratory, along with samples of Terro ant poison.

O'Neal wrapped up his examination of Campbell just before 5:00 P.M., but advised the court that he would be calling him back to the stand later in the trial. The defense announced that they would withhold cross-examination until Campbell had completed his testimony.

When the court recessed for the day, Anjette and her entourage again ran the gauntlet of reporters to reach the relative privacy of the elevator. Moments later, she was back in her cell.

CHAPTER TEN

THE JURORS HAD ONLY A FEW MINUTES TO FRESHEN UP before two deputies rounded them up and escorted them to dinner. They left the courthouse by the back door and walked in single file up the street as one of the lawmen rushed ahead to turn the newspaper boxes around so that none of them could glimpse even a headline. A car full of rowdy young men drove past and shouted at them. The shouts were unintelligible, but the jurors later learned the men had been found and arrested for attempting to tamper with a jury.

At a local steakhouse, the jurors sat around two big tables at the back of the restaurant, separated from the rest of the diners by distance and the watchful eyes of the deputies. After dinner, they were marched back to the courthouse in the cool October twilight. No one complained about the walk. It was a relief to get out of the building and move around. By 7:30, they were in for the night. They passed the evening as best they could—playing cards, talking about anything except the case, and reading the newspapers with large holes where the bailiffs had cut out any reference to the trial.

Wednesday's high temperature was expected to reach the middle eighties. Even with Labor Day a month past, light cottons and short sleeves were the order of the day. As daylight was breaking, the deputies roused their charges and walked them down to the Sears store on Riverside Drive. The jurors were allowed to exercise in the big parking lot there. For most of them, this meant strolling around the paved lot, but a couple did some quick calisthenics before going to a nearby diner for breakfast. The men would have been surprised to learn that the *Macon Telegraph* had run thumbnail sketches of each of them, providing the public with their names, addresses and any other information that had come out during jury selection. As it was, forbidden to read any news of the case, they didn't know about their new celebrity status.

While the jurors ate, crowds of spectators were already forming in the hallway outside the courtroom, filling up all available floor space. The majority of the spectators were women. While the newspaper accounts made much of that fact, putting forth complicated theories of why the trial appealed to one sex more than the other, the explanation may have been as simple as the fact that, in 1958, most women didn't work outside the home and could arrange their days to spend time spent at the courthouse.

More than anything else, people wanted to see Anjette—to watch her face, look at her clothing, to know how she acted in the courtroom. Seeing, and therefore becoming a vicarious part of the notorious case, became almost an obsession for many people. They willingly waited hours on their feet in the hot, crowded hallway for just a glimpse of the defendant. People driving from the north to Florida down US 41 made the side trip to Macon in hopes of seeing some of the action.

Anjette was aware of the acute interest she excited and, as she dressed for court that morning, she knew all eyes would be on her again. She slipped a dark purple dress over her head. It had a high white collar and dainty white cuffs that lent a soft, feminine touch to her appearance. When she walked into the courtroom half an hour later, the spectators watched her closely.

The big room buzzed with conversation. Reporters, quarantined in the balcony, gazed down on the activity below and talked among themselves. As always, Anjette was the topic of conversation. How did she look today? How would you describe her expression? Was that dress purple or plum? Notes were hastily scribbled and the search for new adjectives continued. Since her weight gain, 'glamorous' and 'attractive' had been abandoned in favor of the more ambiguous 'buxom.' There was a stir as Jetta and Alice Donovan entered through the back door. Jetta glared at the people who stared at her, but her daughter-in-law gave the crowd a friendly glance as she took a seat at the defense table. Alice was a pretty woman and today, in a form-fitting shirtwaist dress, dark glasses and big smile, she looked like a minor movie starlet. Unlike Jetta, she didn't seem to mind the cameras.

The first witness of the day was Larry Howard, Assistant Director of the Georgia State Crime Laboratory, who had received the tissue samples from Marcia Lyles's body. Hank O'Neal began his direct examination.

"I received a package through Railway Express containing three jars—two of them containing organs and one containing hair," Howard told the court.

"Who broke the seals on those jars?"

"I did," Howard said.

"Did you analyze these tissues for poison?"

"I did."

"What poison did you find, doctor?"

"I found arsenic," he said matter-of-factly.

O'Neal asked how much arsenic had been found and Howard recited the various milligram levels found in the tissues and hair.

"All right, sir," O'Neal continued, "now tell this jury, are these levels of arsenic which you found sufficient to cause death?"

"Yes, sir. They are many times more than the minimum concentration necessary to cause death."

"How long could a person live with an arsenic level of ten milligrams percent in the liver?"

"Under normal circumstances," Howard said, "you could expect that individual to live from six to twenty-four hours."

The prosecutor paused long enough to let the significance of that answer sink in before asking, "Then I ask you this question: is it possible that a person receiving a fatal dose of arsenic could live for thirty days and still show a level of ten milligrams percent?"

"No. That's impossible."

"Then how could you explain a case where that apparently happened?" O'Neal turned so that he could look directly at Anjette as the pathologist replied.

"The only answer to that would be the fact that multiple doses of arsenic were given, the last dose being administered within three or four days of death."

A murmur arose from the crowd then stilled.

"Was there any indication Marcia Lyles received more than one dose of arsenic?"

"Yes, under multiple administrations, the arsenic tends to accumulate in the fingernails and the hair," the pathologist explained. "And in this case, we have an extremely high level in the hair."

O'Neal handed him a stack of papers and the doctor methodically worked his way through Marcia's hospital records, pointing out the symptoms consistent with arsenic poisoning and giving those in the courtroom an unsettling glimpse of the little girl's anguish during the last month of her life.

"Coughing…constipation…vomiting…here's vomiting with a medium amount of brown fluid mucous."

"Is that significant to you?" O'Neal asked.

"Yes. It indicates the presence of blood in the stomach and, of course, arsenic is a strong irritant." He continued scanning the pages. "Here is some more vomiting. Itching. And here's an indication of irritation of the throat where an ice collar was used. Refused liquids … here the patient was frightened … respiratory congestion … elevated temperature of 104." He laid the papers aside. "I think so far we've been able to find symptoms of respiratory congestion, gastro-intestinal irritation, high temperature, nausea and vomiting and constipated bowel."

Next O'Neal asked Howard about the bodies of Ben Lyles and his mother and Howard described opening the graves and taking the tissue samples from each. Finally he gave a similar description of Buddy Gabbert's exhumation in El Paso.

The jurors, as well as others in the courtroom, shifted in their seats during this testimony. Some exchanged uncomfortable looks. It was one thing for a witness to state that an autopsy had been performed, but quite another to listen as someone described in minute detail the exact procedures for the removal of portions of organs from decaying bodies. Howard gave them more information than most people cared to hear.

Dr. Howard's conclusions as to the causes of death were no surprise. "My opinion is that all four people—Marcia Lyles, Joe Neal Gabbert, Mrs. Ben F. Lyles, Sr. and Ben F. Lyles, Jr., died of arsenic poisoning and further that this arsenic was administered in chronic doses."

Dr. Howard had also tested the Terro ant poison Leonard Campbell sent to the lab.

"It was 94% arsenic," he told the court.

To top off this disturbing testimony, O'Neal approached the witness stand with a handful of photographs. He gave these, one at a time, to Dr. Howard for identification. "Did you, at the time you disinterred the bodies of Ben Lyles, Jr. and Mrs. Ben Lyles, Sr. make any photographs down there, Doctor?"

"Yes, I did."

The first pictures in the stack were of Ben's and Julia's bodies in varying states of decay, positioned formally in their caskets in their tattered funeral clothes. "Now are these the photographs which were made?"

"Yes, sir, they are."

"Are those accurate pictures of the bodies you found there that day?"

Howard nodded. "They are."

"Now let me ask you about some of these other photographs," O'Neal continued. "When you were in the state of Texas, did you take any photographs out there where Mr. Joe Neal Gabbert was buried?"

"I did."

He handed Howard two more photos which the pathologist identified as the outside of Gabbert's casket and one of Gabbert lying inside the open casket.

O'Neal retrieved the photos and handed them to William Buffington at the defense table for his consideration. Her three lawyers took their time examining the photos, but Anjette didn't look at them.

Next the photographs were marked as prosecution exhibits and, finally, passed to the jury. The courtroom was silent as each juror gazed at the grisly images before handing them on to the next man. One or two of them couldn't suppress a grimace.

Buffington's cross examination of Dr. Howard had been eagerly anticipated by some of the press who were familiar with the crime lab man's cool demeanor under pressure. Since the defense attorney had quite a reputation of his own, serious fireworks were expected. The encounter was disappointing. Except for a minor skirmish over the focus in some of the photographs, the questioning was unremarkable and did nothing to further the defense's cause.

As soon as the morning recess was called, Anjette slipped through a rear door, deputy in tow. She found a moment's privacy in the back hall and smoked a quick cigarette.

On the other side of the building, outside the main entrance, the corridor had been filling with people all morning. In the sea of femininity, a man could be spotted here and there. One elderly gentleman leaned heavily on a cane, looking as if it were all that stood between him and total collapse. During the recess, a deputy stepped out of the courtroom and announced that there were a few empty seats inside. The aimless milling stopped and people rushed the door. A few lucky ones managed to push inside, including the elderly man who slipped nimbly past the others, the unnecessary cane tipped jauntily over his shoulder.

One of the jurors, H. D. Murrell took the break as an opportunity to notify a bailiff that he was sick. He hadn't been well the night before and his condition had worsened during the morning. Judge Long did not challenge him. He was excused from the trial and Mackey Clark, an alternate, took his place when the case resumed.

Dr. Robert Ireland was a handsome man with a high forehead and a small, neat mustache that gave him the look of a silent screen idol. He had been Marcia Lyles's attending physician. Like the witness before him, he went into great medical detail about the child's condition. But his most sensational testimony concerned Anjette's reaction during the period of time when Marcia had experienced significant improvement.

"Now when this child made this dramatic improvement, did you tell anybody the good news?" O'Neal asked.

"Of course. I told her mother."

"What was the reaction of Mrs. Anjette Lyles?"

"Entirely opposite to what I expected. I had been very encouraged, but when I passed on the news, Mrs. Lyles just seemed to accept it without too much emotional display. She said, 'Well, it can't last much longer. She is going to get worse again.' It was very discouraging to me because all of us had worked quite hard on the case."

"'It can't last much longer. She will get worse.' Is that what she said?" O'Neal asked.

"Words to that effect."

"Now, Dr. Ireland, the improvement, did that last very long?"

"It did not—a matter of two days or so."

William Buffington's cross examination of Robert Ireland was lengthy and repetitious. Using the doctor's own notes from the hospital charts, he led him through a second recital of Marcia Lyles's symptoms and spent several minutes exploring other possible illnesses that could cause similar symptoms. Dr. Ireland dismissed, in turn, the possibility that Marcia died of leukemia, aplastic anemia or encephalitis.

Buffington returned to the defense table and selected a piece of paper from a stack there. "All right, sir. Now, on March 26, 1958, did you write a progress report saying Marcia was 'at death's door last night. Every evidence of complete bone marrow suppression'?"

"That's correct."

"So doctor, your feelings did go beyond just the possibility of death, didn't they?"

"I'm sure I felt at times that the patient would die."

"These reports, they are available so nurses can see them, are they not?"

"Yes, they are," Ireland answered.

"Do you know whether or not any nurse conveyed what was written in this report to Mrs. Lyles?"

"I do not."

Buffington nodded with some satisfaction and Ireland was released.

"Look at her," a woman a few rows behind the defense table whispered to her friend, loud enough for Anjette to hear. "She doesn't react to anything. I've never seen a woman so *cold*."

The prosecution called Latrelle West to the witness stand.

After the attractive young secretary was settled in the wooden chair and had sworn to tell the truth, Hank O'Neal had her explain how she had come to spend the evening of May 6 with Anjette.

"I was placed on guard at the hospital room with Mrs. Lyles."

"Had you been sent there for any other purpose than to act as a guard, such purpose as attempting to frame or prod this defendant into saying anything?"

"No." She seemed a bit offended by the suggestion.

After describing Anjette as "laughing and joking," West related parts of the conversation she'd had with Anjette that night. She told how Anjette had declared she'd never received any money from Buddy Gabbert's death.

O'Neal turned to the jury to make sure they took note of that. "She got nothing?"

"That's right."

"Now, was there any conversation at all about her first husband, Ben Lyles, Jr.?"

"Yes, she talked about him, too. She said that she should have had an autopsy performed on him, but he had always wanted to be cremated, but Mrs. Lyles pitched a fit and wouldn't let her have him cremated, but that she should have had him cremated."

"Did she state to you whether or not she received any financial benefit for the death of Ben F. Lyles, Jr., known as Little Ben?"

"She said she did not receive anything."

Again he looked at the jurors, willing them to understand.

"She's twisting what I said," Anjette whispered to Buffington. He gestured with a hand for her to be quiet.

"Was there any discussion at the time you were there of any insurance benefits or any possible insurance benefits that might in the future accrue to the defendant Anjette Lyles?" the prosecutor asked.

"Well, she asked me would she not collect double on their lives if she was cleared."

"What did you reply to that?"

"I told her that I didn't know if the policy had a double indemnity clause in there or not. I didn't know whether she would or not. She said, well usually policies did have the double indemnity clause and, if she was cleared, she would collect double on their lives."

This prompted another wave of whispering, but it stopped as quickly as it had begun. No one wanted to miss a word spoken from the witness stand.

"While you were there, did Mrs. Lyles have a visitor come to that room?" O'Neal asked.

"Yes, sir. Dr. Ireland came in and Mr. Buffington came."

"Mr. Buffington? That gentleman sitting right over there?"

"Yes, sir. When he came in, he told her he'd talked to the news reporters and had told them that she said she had committed no crime. And that would be what she would say from then on," West continued. "She'd say, 'I have committed no crime.'"

"During the time you spent with her, did Mrs. Lyles make any statement with reference to any possible help that might be available to her?"

"Yes, sir. She said all the brass hats in Macon would be behind her and she stated she had a letter that would clear her of all these charges. She said it would burn them up; that it would clear her of the charges against her."

"I see," O'Neal said slowly. "Did she say whose handwriting that letter was in?"

"She stated it was Mrs. Lyles's handwriting."

William Buffington glanced at Anjette and she could tell he wasn't happy about her having talked to Latrelle West. He had told her days before the arrest not to say anything about the case to anyone.

"Now where did she say she got that letter from?"

"Well, she said one day she needed a black pocketbook and she wanted to use one of Mrs. Lyles's, and she asked the maid to get it for her and the maid got the pocketbook to clean out the contents for her to use. And the maid found a split in the lining and said, 'Miss Anjette, here's a piece of paper.' Well, the maid gave it to her and it was a letter written to her from Mrs. Lyles. She said this letter upset her so bad she gave it to Mr. Buffington to keep, and that they had some photostatic copies made of it."

William Buffington stood to cross examine Latrelle West. He smiled as he walked toward the witness stand, and Anjette slid forward an inch or two in her seat, eager to see him set Latrelle West straight. But the attorney seemed to have been stung by the witness's words and was intent on restoring his own image.

"Mrs. West, this was the afternoon that she was arrested that you are relating to, is it not?"

"Yes."

"Now, you recall when I got there, kind of late that night, my having commented to you that I had been over in Harris County, Georgia? And that I had just got in?"

"Yes, sir."

"Didn't I also make comments that I knew the arrest was taking place even though I was in Harris County?"

"I don't remember," she said.

"All right. You do not know that I hadn't told her one, two or three days later what comment she was to make if she was served with any warrant?"

"No, I don't."

"Well, you didn't think anything strange about an attorney giving a client some advice, did you?"

"No, I didn't."

"And it is right normal for a lawyer to advise his client if he sees fit? And from your observations down there in the Sheriff's office, Mrs. West, isn't it quite common for the client to ask the lawyer, 'what should I say'?"

"Yes."

"Just one other thing, Mrs. West, when she purportedly made this statement that all the brass — I don't want to misquote you now — all the brass hats of Macon would be behind her, she wasn't referring to me, was she?"

"I don't know who she was referring to."

"All right. Now about this letter. Did she go into the contents of this letter that you say she gave to me?"

"She said it was a letter from Mrs. Lyles apologizing to her, to Anjette, for what—for something that she had done to her. In other words, something that Mrs. Lyles had done to her. It was an apology."

Buffington thanked the witness and Latrelle West left the stand.

The court broke for lunch around noon and Anjette returned to her cell under the dome. From somewhere in the jail below came the sound of a radio being played loud. She could make out the exuberant strains of "Volare." She'd always liked that song, even though the Italian lyrics meant nothing to her. The lilting melody always raised her spirits and today she certainly could use that. She tapped one foot to the music and waited for her lunch.

CHAPTER ELEVEN

WHEN COURT RESUMED AND O'NEAL CALLED J. TAYLOR PHIL-
lips, the drowsy after-lunch crowd perked up. Phillips was an important
man in Macon, an up-and-coming attorney who had won the Demo-
cratic primary election in September for state representative. His winning the seat in the general election was taken for granted, since in the
1950s Republicans were little more than curiosities in Georgia, seldom
seen or heard from, and never factors in any election.

His prominence had made his involvement in the case a topic for
speculation for months. The burning question was what exactly his and
Anjette's relationship had been. Of course there had been the same talk
about every other man who was even remotely associated with her.

The young politician took the stand and responded to Hank
O'Neal's opening question by stating his profession as attorney at law.

The prosecutor shared a small smile with the jury. "Did you get into
some other occupation this past summer?"

"Yes, sir. I ran for the House of Representatives."

"Got in politics?"

"Yes, sir."

Phillips acknowledged that he knew both Anjette and her second
husband, Buddy Gabbert. He had been, he told the jury, a pallbearer
at his funeral.

"Did you know him well?"

"I suppose I was as close as anyone. He was a real friendly sort of
fellow, real likable, but he was in town so little. About the only place I
saw him was up at the restaurant. Really, my friendship for him was
through Anjette."

O'Neal had Phillips describe his time as a patient at Parkview
Hospital. He'd been treated for pneumonia the same time Buddy
Gabbert had been hospitalized there.

"Mrs. Anjette Lyles came down to see me when she found out I was there. She mentioned that her husband was a patient there also and that she thought a will would be a good idea. Now whether it was in a kidding way or not, I don't know."

"Did you act on that suggestion of the defendant?"

"I got up—I was up at the time, sitting on the side of the bed with my bathrobe on and bedroom shoes—and walked down to Buddy's room, which was just a short way around the corner of the hall. I tried to talk with him, but Buddy was in such bad shape that it was just impossible. You know, he was scaly looking and his mouth looked like it was all broken out, like it was difficult for him to even talk, so I didn't talk or anything else except say 'I hope you get to feeling better' and then I left."

"Mr. Phillips, I wish you would go a little more into detail for the jury about the actual condition of that man."

Phillips frowned a bit at the memory. "Well, his eyes were extremely red. The scale was up all around his eyes and around his nose and even around his beard. He kept scratching at himself and he seemed to be in intense pain. It is difficult to describe pain, but his physical appearance was ... scaly, scratchy, miserable. He seemed kind of out of his head, too. When you talked to him, he just didn't seem to make much coherent sense."

O'Neal took off in another direction. "Let me ask you some questions relative to Mrs. Ben Lyles, Sr. Several months before she died, did you have occasion to be in Anjette Lyles's restaurant when any discussion occurred with reference to Mrs. Lyles?"

"Yes."

"At that time, did Anjette Lyles show you anything?"

Phillips nodded. "She had two bank books on two different federal savings banks in Atlanta. They were in Mrs. Lyles's name, not Anjette Lyles, but her mother-in-law. The amounts in those books totaled between eighty and ninety thousand dollars, giving me the impression Mrs. Lyles was pretty well to do."

"And in whose possession were those books when they were showed to you?"

"In Anjette Lyles'."

"And how long was that before the death of Mrs. Lyles?"

"I'd say anywhere from four to six months."

Phillips also related the conversation he and Anjette had concerning Julia's reluctance to make a will.

"Did you have anything to do with drawing a will for her?"

"No, sir."

"Now make this plain, if you will, Mr. Phillips. Was that in a public place where this conversation happened?"

"It was in the restaurant there. We were drinking coffee—we usually drink coffee up there every day—and there were a whole bunch of people around."

"There was no private conference about it?"

"No, sir. No, sir."

O'Neal then asked if Phillips had visited Anjette in the hospital shortly before her arrest.

"Yes, sir. I had reasonable good suspicion that a warrant was going to be taken out for her. I did go up to visit her, I believe on a Tuesday, and told her that in my opinion, some murder warrants were going to be taken for her. I was not there as an attorney, but we had been good friends and I was up there simply to let her know what was going to happen."

"Did you tell her that she had better take any steps of any kind?"

"I told her I thought it would be a good idea, if she was not guilty, to get herself a couple of good lawyers and not to say anything to anybody about this case except what her lawyers told her to say. I told her I was not for hire in the case. I was just up there to tell her what I thought she ought to do, strictly not any attorney-client business."

"Was anything said about any kind of poison?"

"Yes. When I told her that a warrant would be taken, she asked if it was about Marcia. And I told her yes, that she probably had heard the rumors, too, that warrants were going to be taken. And at that time, she said, 'Well, my maid has seen Marcia drinking some Terro ant poison out at the house and probably that's the way that arsenic got in her blood or wherever it got.'"

"That's the way the arsenic got into Marcia's body, is that what the defendant said?"

"That's right."

O'Neal was still asking questions. "Following that, were you shown any papers up there, Mr. Phillips?"

"Yes, Anjette showed me a photostat of a letter that she claimed Mrs. Lyles had written before her death."

"Did you read that letter?"

"Yes, sir. I read it twice. It was addressed to Anjette and it was signed Julia Lyles."

"Did she state to you anything that the letter would accomplish?"

"She said it would show she had nothing to do with Little Ben's death or Mrs. Lyles's death because in the letter it stated—in a rather indirect sort of way, I thought—that Mrs. Lyles was the one responsible for her own death plus her son's death."

"What did you do with that photostat after you read it?"

"I handed it back to her."

"Was that the last you ever saw of it?"

"Yes, sir."

William Buffington handled the cross examination of Phillips as he had all of the others to this point.

"Now, Mr. Phillips, when do you consider was the last time that you actually represented Anjette in any sort of matter?"

"Last time I represented her, I believe, was when I had her name changed back from Gabbert to Lyles."

"And you recall roughly how soon after Gabbert's death that was?"

"It was within a year, I am reasonably sure."

"And you don't recall actually representing her any since that particular time?"

"No, sir."

Buffington sighed and looked at the jury box as if the men there shared his exasperation.

"Now, Mr. Phillips, I believe you did testify on direct examination that when she mentioned something about Buddy maybe needed a will, it may have been in a joking manner, she might have been kidding?"

"I just don't recall. She came down—I thought to see me—and yet all she talked about was that, so I just don't know. I mean, she asked me how I was feeling and I asked her how Buddy was feeling and she said that he wasn't doing so well, said he ought to have a will. And we kind of laughed about that, you know. Anybody that's sick and you talk about a will, I always consider it joking, really, more than anything."

"Well, she always joked and laughed with you in the restaurant over there. Was this something similar to that sort of conversation?" Buffington asked.

"No, I wouldn't—It was merely my impression. She could have been serious or she couldn't have been. But she mentioned it and I got up and we went down to his room."

Buffington nodded, satisfied with the answer. He returned to the reason Phillips had visited Anjette in the hospital.

"I felt like Anjette and I had been pretty good friends at one time and I ought to go up there and tell her what was going to happen and tell her to get some lawyers and take their advice. I know that she is subject to talk a little bit too much. And sometimes she might say something that people can misconstrue. And frequently—you and I both know—clients will say things they shouldn't say that don't mean a thing. I was just doing what I did as a friend, that's all."

"So you're telling us that in the past she talked about frivolous things to you and that those things might have been misconstrued by others?"

"That's right."

Then Buffington entered territory that, in retrospect, he would wish he had avoided. He returned to the subject of the letter.

"How was the letter signed? Was there a middle initial?"

"It was signed Julia Lyles. Whether or not there was a middle initial, I don't remember."

"Had you, prior to that time, ever seen the signature of Mrs. Julia Lyles?"

"Yes, oh, yes."

"I'll ask you whether or not on that photostatic copy that you saw, you thought it was some similar to the signature."

Phillips paused a second or two before answering. "Yes, there was a similarity—a slight similarity. But it didn't look to me like her signature."

Buffington left the subject then, but the damage had been done.

O'Neal could hardly wait for the cross examination to end. As soon as Buffington headed back to the defense table, Hank was on his feet ready to march through the door that had been eased open by the defense.

"I believe Mr. Buffington asked you a while ago something about your opinion of the validity of the signature on that letter, didn't he?"

"Yes, sir."

"Now, I ask you, Mr. Witness, did you form any opinion at that time whether that was a valid signature or not?"

"Yes, sir," Taylor answered. "I formed an opinion it was not valid."

"That it was, in fact, what?"

"A forgery."

O'Neal knew when to quit. He released the witness, confident the jury would remember Phillips's last words.

William Hutchinson was the prosecution's next witness. He was a construction worker, a "good ole boy" in the best sense of the word, who seemed completely out of place on the witness stand. He had become involved in the state's most notorious murder case only because his wife had been a waitress at Anjette's Restaurant. Watching him fidget in the chair, his tie seeming too tight for comfort, Anjette couldn't imagine why they'd called Bill to testify.

"Did your wife formerly work for the defendant, Anjette Donovan Lyles?"

"Yes, sir."

"Now what time would she get off at night from her employment there at the restaurant?"

"Well, nine o'clock was closing time, so anywhere between nine and ten."

"Would you ever go down there to get your wife to bring her home?" O'Neal asked.

"Every night."

"Every night? So were you in that restaurant frequently?"

"I'd say over fifty percent of the time I went after her I went inside."

"All right. Now when you would go in that restaurant, I wonder if you ever saw a child there by the name of Marcia?"

"Many times."

"Did you ever have occasion to see any of the dealings between Anjette Lyles and her daughter, Marcia?"

"I did." In a voice unaccustomed to public speaking, Hutchinson described a particular time when Marcia was asking Anjette for something. "I don't remember what she wanted, but she come to her about two times and Mrs. Lyles told her to go on outside or something.

Then she came back and asked her again and Mrs. Lyles taken the child by the arm and shook her and taken her over and sit her down in the booth and cursed her."

"Now tell the jury what she said. Tell this jury what the defendant called that child."

Hutchinson cleared his throat. "Well, she called her a little Lyles-looking son of a bitch. Told her if she didn't set down and behave, she would kill her."

"A little Lyles-looking son of a bitch," O'Neal repeated for the benefit of the jury. "Now, Mr. Witness, did any of you all say anything to this defendant about having talked to the child in that manner?"

"Yes, sir. A couple of us, we talked to her and told her we didn't think she meant that and she shouldn't talk to the child that way."

"And what did she say back to you?"

"She said she did mean it."

"Did you ever see any other occasion similar to that ?"

"Yes, sir," Hutchinson confirmed. "There was one other. She grabbed the child and shook her and took her back in the kitchen."

"Did she curse her?"

"Yes, she went back in the kitchen and—I don't remember exactly the words she said, but —"

"Was it some rough language?"

"Yes, it was rough language."

Buffington tried to minimize the damage on cross examination.

"How many children you got?"

"Two girls," Hutchinson answered. "Four and seven."

"Now you went down there as you indicated a good many times to pick up your wife, didn't you?"

"That's right."

"And can you give us any idea, Mr. Hutchinson, what year this was supposed to have happened in?"

"What year?" The witness sounded surprised by the question.

"Yes, sir."

"Well, it was the first of this year, I suppose," Hutchinson said uncertainly.

"Well, now, let's don't 'suppose', Mr. Hutchinson," Buffington said testily. "Let's testify like you know."

"And uh —- "

"Was it this year or last year?"

"It was this year *and* last year. I'd say it is my testimony, I mean about the child, was, I'd say it was in two to three month's before the child's death."

"Two to three months?"

"Yes, sir, before the child's death."

"Well, do you know when the child died?"

"I don't remember the exact date now, but—I don't even remember the *month* now," the harried witness said, eliciting some sympathetic chuckles from the courtroom.

"Well, sir, now just what—Were you all sitting around in a booth when this transpired?"

"That's right."

"And what did the child ask for?"

"I don't remember. I wasn't paying any attention to her at that time."

"Well, what was the child doing?" Buffington persisted.

"She was running back and forth from the front outside the restaurant back in to her mother."

Buffington changed tactics and approached Hutchinson one parent to another. "Was Marcia kind of being annoying at that time?"

The witness agreed that maybe she was. Buffington pressed the point. "They kind of get you upset every now and then, don't they?"

"Well, I suppose it's possible for kids to upset their parents," the witness said cautiously.

"Depending on how hard a day you had and just how bad you felt when you got in as to what sort of conduct would make you a little peeved, wouldn't it?"

"Peeved" was probably not a word that came easily to William Hutchinson's lips. He decided to cut through the confusion and bring the speculation to a quick close. "Well, I believe I'd go cut me a switch."

"That's a good instrument," Buffington said with a smile. "I take it from what you said that her conduct was such that, if she had been yours, you would have went out and cut you a little switch and used it?"

Hutchinson nodded.

"Well, now, on that particular occasion, was her conduct such that you would have switched her?"

"I don't say on this same occasion I would have, but I've seen plenty of times I would have switched her if she had been mine. I've seen the time they needed it, but didn't get it; maybe when their grandmother was there. Something like that."

Buffington moved on. "Did you ever see any candles burning down there at that restaurant?"

Before the witness could answer, the prosecution objected. It wasn't until Buffington assured the court that the information was not intended to help construct an insanity defense that Hutchinson was allowed to answer.

"Yes, sir, I did."

"You know what sort of candles they were?"

"Well, I don't *know* what—I only heard her say what they was for. Green one I heard was for good luck and, I guess, the red one, I think that was for some kind of romance. I don't know." He was embarrassed to be repeating such foolishness.

On redirect, O'Neal pursued the subject. "Mr. Witness, you know what color candle you burn that signifies the fact you are supposed to get a whole lot of money?"

Hutchinson shook his head. "No, sir, I don't believe I do."

"Can you tell this jury what burning a black candle means to people that believe in them?"

"I understand that it means death."

O'Neal sat down and Buffington stood up again. By now Bill Hutchinson was wondering if they were ever going to let him leave.

"Now what color candles did you see burning in the restaurant?"

"As I stated, the only colors I can remember are green and red."

"Do you know very much about that sort of stuff."

"No, sir, I do not."

"Now this black candle Mr. O'Neal was talking about, do you know whether that is supposed to predict a death or something?"

"Suppose to be asking for death, I understand. Wanting a death. Wanting somebody to die. But I don't know. I'm no authority on that, I'll tell you right now."

The last answer was stated with such conviction that even Judge Long joined in the resulting laughter.

Finally Hutchinson was released and O'Neal called Billy Gene Davis, another man whose wife had worked for Anjette. He was no more comfortable in the courtroom than Bill Hutchinson had been. He, too, had been in the habit of going into the restaurant when picking up his wife.

"Did you see any dealings between Mrs. Anjette Donovan Lyles and this child Marcia?"

"Yes, sir. On this particular night that I remember, I was with my brother-in-law, Bill Hutchinson. We went in to pick his wife up and we were sitting in the booth, and the kid was up at the front by the cash register. I believe she was wanting money, a quarter or fifty cents to buy a present or something with. And Mrs. Lyles, she come up the aisle from the back and told her she'd kill her if it was the last thing she ever did do if she didn't shut up."

O'Neal repeated the threat for the jury. "Did you see that child do anything worse than ask for a quarter?"

"No, sir, I didn't."

As Davis left the witness stand, the jury and spectators had time to reflect on a nine-year-old child cursed and threatened with death by her mother, the same child who, only a few months later, died a painful and terrifying death.

CHAPTER TWELVE

WEDNESDAY AFTERNOON WORE ON.

"How much longer will the trial go on?" Anjette asked Buffington. She felt like she'd already spent a lifetime in this courtroom. His only answer was a shrug and a shake of his head.

O'Neal and Adams had arrived at the point in the trial where the financial motive for the murders would be laid out. The testimony was vital, but was sure to be less than exciting. By calling a parade of witnesses, the prosecution presented evidence that Anjette had collected life insurance benefits from the deaths of her husbands totaling $23,000. There had also been a small policy on Marcia's life, but benefits had never been paid on that one since the beneficiary had been arrested.

After William George, district manager for Metropolitan Life Insurance Company, had testified about his company's policy on Joe Neal Gabbert, William Buffington questioned him about the medical examination his company had required Buddy to take.

"Do you have that report there?"

George shuffled through the papers. "Yes. This is the doctor's examination here."

"Where he was examined by Dr. Ferrell?"

"Right."

"Can you read this, Mr. George?" Buffington indicated a section of the medical report.

"Yes. Question is, had the applicant ever been treated for any skin or gland disease. The answer is: yes, has a slight irritation of the skin. Appears to be a mild form of eczema."

"And that is signed by Dr. Ferrell on August 2, 1955?"

"That's right."

"So from that medical report, he had a rash on him some four months before your proof of death was filed?" Buffington asked.

"That's right."

The attorney smiled at the jury and released the witness.

Next Lewis Smith, a Macon real estate agent, told the court how he had handled the sale of Julia Lyles's house for Anjette.

"As a result of that sale, what was the figure that was eventually paid to the seller?"

"Six thousand seven hundred and seventy nine dollars."

"Did your company prepare a check in that amount?"

"We did, sir." He held up the paper for the jury to see. "It was payable to Anjette D. Lyles, Executrix, under the will of Mrs. Julia Lyles."

Charles Adams got his first opportunity to question witnesses that afternoon. He wished the testimony were more interesting. As one person followed another on the stand, heads began to droop in the courtroom and spectators moved in their seats to counteract drowsiness. Legs were crossed, recrossed and discreetly stretched. One of the jurors popped a cough drop into his mouth, then passed the box among his fellow panelists.

When Adams called Ernest Lee, vice president of the First National Bank, he began trying to make good his partner's earlier promise to prove that Anjette spent money like a drunken sailor.

Lee testified to Anjette's history with his bank, beginning in April of 1955. There was no doubt she'd been in bad financial shape just after Buddy's death.

"What was the balance in her account in January of 1956?"

Lee consulted a ledger card. "Balance in the account on January 31, 1956, was $7.19."

But by the middle of February, thanks to the proceeds from Gabbert's insurance and veterans' benefits, that balance had swelled to over $20,000. With Lee's help, Adams gave the jury a glimpse of Anjette's spending habits.

"Now, what was the balance in that account at the close of February?"

"$8,588.96."

"What was in there at the close of April?"

"$244.14," Lee answered.

"Say that again, please."

"$244.14."

Adams shook his head at the small figure.

The First National Bank had also made a business loan to Anjette in April of 1955 in the amount of $8,000 and Lee recounted the history of that loan. There were numerous instances of late payments. In fact the bank had never received a payment on the loan that wasn't at least a few days late, and they had found it necessary at one time to lend her additional money to prevent her from defaulting.

Finally Adams asked about an account opened by Anjette, in the amount of $9,404, in her capacity as executrix of Julia Lyles's estate.

"I hand you here the ten checks that are written to Anjette Lyles, as guardian of either Marcia or Carla Lyles, and ask you just to—if you can read on the back of those, who those checks were endorsed by? Can you make out that writing?"

"This looks like Rosemary Reynolds. Next one is William Donovan. Next one is William Donovan. Next one is Parkview Hospital. Next one by Mulberry Provision Company. Ethel Bean. This is endorsed W. G. Wilson. This is endorsed Ethel Bean. This one Mrs. Ethel Bean. And this by Mrs. Leila ... looks like Rondlein."

At the end of an hour, Lee was as glad to leave the witness stand as the people in the courtroom were to hear the last of the dry testimony about checks and deposits and loan payments. His place was taken a few minutes later by Ivan Parragin of the Veterans Administration. He testified that Buddy Gabbert had made Anjette the beneficiary of his National Service life insurance in October of 1955.

"All right, sir," Hank O'Neal said. "Now is there, in your file, any inquiry during the month of June 1955, about whether or not this insurance was in force?"

The witness looked at the papers he held. "Yes, sir. On June 21. It's right here."

"I don't want to confuse you on these dates, but does your file reveal when this woman," he indicated Anjette with a jerk of his head, "married Mr. Joe Neal Gabbert?"

"Yes, sir, it does. June 25, 1955."

"June 25? So this inquiry about insurance was made three days before the marriage?"

"Yes, sir."

"Will you read it to us?" O'Neal requested.

"This letter is on a letterhead showing Lone Star Motel & Grill, U. S. Highway 80, Pecos, Texas. Dated Pecos, Texas, June 21, 1955, directed to Veterans Administration District Office."

"Can you read the body of it?"

"'Federal Center, Denver, Colorado. Please advise me if my policy is still in force or elapsed. Seems like I have not received a premium notice for some time. I believe the last premium was paid in February. Please advise and send notice.' That's all. It bears the signature 'J. N. Gabbert.'"

"Are there other papers in the file signed by Joe Neal Gabbert?"

"Yes, sir. Quite a number of letters and forms."

When Parragin explained that he'd turned over all the papers bearing Gabbert's signature to Mrs. Mary Beacom at the Georgia State Crime Lab, William Buffington jumped to his feet.

"Your honor, I object! The defense has not had sufficient time to examine the Veterans Administration file."

"There has been plenty of opportunity for Mr. Buffington or anyone else the defense chose to examine the documents while they were in Atlanta," O'Neal countered.

The argument continued until, maneuvered by Judge Long's steady hand, a compromise was reached. The state would make photostatic copies of all the documents and give them to the defense team for examination and O'Neal assured the court that the papers wouldn't be introduced as evidence until the next day.

It was after 5:00 P.M. and the jurors were growing restless. Several of them moved around in their seats and glanced meaningfully at their watches, but Judge Long paid them no attention and instructed the prosecution to call their next witness.

John Henry West, an Oldsmobile dealer from nearby Warner Robins, told the court that Anjette was shopping for a white convertible during the summer of 1957.

"I had a white convertible and it was a nice looking car—solid white, white top, trimmed on the inside. I told Mrs. Lyles about it when she called, and I brought that particular automobile in and showed it to Mrs. Lyles—Mrs. Lyles, Jr. I parked the car on Mulberry Street and went into the restaurant."

He identified Anjette, expressionless at the defense table, as the woman he'd talked to on that summer afternoon. He went on to explain that she had wanted to buy the car that day, but, even with the trade-in of her own vehicle, she couldn't afford the Oldsmobile.

"I told her it would take a minimum of one thousand dollars down payment to buy it."

"Now tell this jury, what did the defendant tell you then?" O'Neal prompted.

"She said that a month or so from then she could pay the thousand dollars or probably could pay cash for the automobile. She mentioned that Mrs. Ben Lyles, Sr., was in the hospital and I remarked something along the line that I hoped it wasn't anything serious, but she said, yes, she thought that it was serious and didn't think Mrs. Lyles would pull through."

"Did she assign any reason as to why she would be able to pay cash for the automobile?"

"Well, yes, sir," West said. "She said she and her children were beneficiaries under Mrs. Lyles's will."

That statement roused a number of spectators and whispering broke out in the big room. Judge Long silenced it with a frown.

Jack Gautier cross-examined West and tried unsuccessfully to shake the car dealer's identification of Anjette, pointing out that most of their conversations were by telephone. But the man on the witness stand wouldn't give an inch and stuck by his original identification.

Macon banker W. M. Parker was the last witness of the day. Vice president of the City Bank & Trust Company, he took the stand with an armload of bank records. There was an almost audible collective sigh. No one there was pleased to discover they were about to be subjected to more financial testimony. Even people who had waited hours to get seats in the audience were ready to call it a day.

Charles Adams approached the witness. "Mr. Parker, did your bank have an account listed under the name of the Estate of Mrs. Julia D. Young Lyles?"

"Yes, sir."

"What was the original deposit?"

"$327.64. Then in November of 1957, there were additional deposits."

The banker seemed ready to read those figures, but Adams asked, "In round figures, Mr. Parker, without being exact, what would the approximate amount of those deposits be?"

"About thirty-four or thirty-five hundred dollars."

"And what was the balance on that account at the end of December?"

"$262.84."

"And now will you go to January?"

"The balance January 21 was $9.84."

As he'd done with the other banker, Adams had Parker list the checks drawn on the account. The majority of those checks had been made out to Anjette Lyles, Executrix. These, in turn, carried a variety of endorsements: the Mulberry Provision Company, two to Mrs. Robert Almond, several to a local liquor store, several to Gladys Bryan, two to Hugh Dennis Tire Company, and one to Jetta Donovan. The rest had been endorsed by Anjette alone and deposited in her own account. After a few minutes, the recitation of figures became an almost unintelligible drone to the weary jurors. When Judge Long finally recessed for the day at one minute before seven, one of the jurors muttered "It's about time."

CHAPTER THIRTEEN

THE REPORTERS STRAGGLED OUT INTO THE TWILIGHT, BLINK-
ing like people leaving a movie theater for the reality of everyday life.
By the end of this third day of trial, they had become so preoccupied
with Anjette and the murders that it took them several minutes to re-
connect with the outside world. As they made their way along the
sidewalks, passersby who recognized them as news people asked about
the trial and more specifically about the defendant. How did she look?
Had she said anything? Did she seem sorry or upset? On a day when
the world mourned the death of Pope Pius XXIII and sports-minded
folks across the country eagerly followed a World Series with New York
and Milwaukee tied at three games each, Macon's only concern seemed
to be murder.

Anjette kicked off her black pumps as soon as she returned to her
cell. She couldn't remember ever being so tired. It was exhausting to sit
still, never saying a word, while people came forward, one after
another, and said things that made you sound like a terrible person.

About 7:30 P.M., Byrice brought her a tray. She poured Coke over
ice and sipped it.

"Byrice, they're making it sound like I spent the money on me—just
me—and never did anything for my girls. Now you know that's not
true."

Byrice sat beside her on the small bed and put an arm around her
shoulders. "I know, honey. Try not to let it get you down."

The two women were quiet. There seemed to be little to talk about
that night.

Ollie Goings had often described Judge Oscar Long as "a gentleman
in every sense of the word," and that Wednesday evening, the judge
showed just how considerate he could be. He suspected the jurors were
in for several more long days, so he made a telephone call and
arranged a small treat for them. After a late dinner, the thirteen men

and the ever-present deputies walked the short distance to the Grand Theater where the manager unlocked the doors and ushered them into the lobby. Once all the lights had been turned on, the deputies walked through the theater, checking every row of seats to make sure no one was hidden there. When they had satisfied themselves that the whole place, including the balcony, was empty, the jurors were marched in. The lights dimmed and the projectionist ran a movie, "Harry Black and the Tiger," for this exclusive audience. For a couple of hours, the men lost themselves in the jungles of India with Stewart Granger, exotic women and man-eating beasts. Later that night, as each juror settled into his small cot, he had something to reflect on other than Anjette Lyles.

Thursday was another warm day and the old courthouse on Mulberry Street was overwhelmed once more by a crush of people, each one hoping to claim a coveted courtroom seat.

Anjette took her accustomed place and glanced casually to her left where the men who eventually would decide her guilt or innocence were settling in for the fourth day of the trial. None of them met her gaze. Anjette's throat was sore and her head was becoming stuffy. She pulled a handkerchief from her handbag and held it in her hand.

Dr. Richard Ford, the Massachusetts expert who'd taught O'Neal and Adams so much about arsenic poisoning, was the day's first witness. He was a tall, thin, almost skeletal man who answered questions in a deep voice with a sprinkling of dry wit. O'Neal first had to qualify him as an expert. By the time he finished listing his qualifications and accomplishments in that confident New England drawl, no one doubted that Ford was an expert.

O'Neal had him describe the general effects of some common poisons and with familiar detachment the pathologist related the unpleasant results of ingesting such things as cyanide and carbolic acid. Then the testimony turned to arsenic.

"Arsenic is a great imitator," Ford declared.

"Explain that to the jury. What do you mean by imitator?"

"What I mean is that arsenic poisoning can imitate so many other physical complaints that, unless the physician is forewarned, he will, in almost all cases, not make the diagnosis."

Ford explained that the poison had no characteristic odor and that its taste could be masked easily by mixing it with another substance.

"Is it likely that arsenic could be administered in small doses?" O'Neal asked.

"In the use of this poison for homicidal purposes, that is the usual procedure. A single great big dose frequently causes vomiting, so the dose is lost. But if repeated small doses are given, the body picks up this lethal chemical, stores it and the damage is done."

The prosecution then introduced into evidence the medical records of each of the four victims. They were admitted by Judge Long, over Jack Gautier's now familiar objection.

O'Neal handed the stack of records to the witness. "Dr. Ford, do you recognize these records?"

"Yes. I finished reading those at 4:15 this morning." He raised an eyebrow. "Word by word."

Taking the records one victim at a time, paraphrasing the symptoms of each and reading from the records the varying amounts of arsenic found in the bodies, O'Neal asked for Ford's conclusions.

Ford never hesitated. The deaths of all the victims, he declared, were due to arsenic poisoning, administered over a period of time.

O'Neal had a final point to make. "Doctor, you say that the poison would have to have been given over a long period of time. Can you tell the jury why you say that?"

"I can say it in one word: fingernails."

O'Neal chuckled. "That's a little too short."

Ford nodded. "Well, we all know the rate that fingernails grow. We have to cut them. There was arsenic in the fingernails of all the victims. The only way that arsenic gets into the fingernails is by the place where the nail grows under the cuticle, under the skin. Their fingernails, whole fingernails, were full of arsenic. They won't pick it up like that unless it has been given over a long period of time."

William Buffington didn't fare well taking on the pathologist. Ford, he discovered, considered cross-examination something of a sport and a sport at which he excelled.

"Doctor, you say you're from Boston?" He made it sound like he was asking if Ford were from Mars.

"I am."

"Now all this cyanide and these other multiple varieties of poisons that you testified to, do those people up there in Massachusetts take that stuff?"

"We have our fair share of fools and villains, too," Ford said dryly, provoking some appreciative smiles.

"Have you had a great deal of experience in seeing those people that have took that stuff you testified about?"

"Well, in my part of Boston alone I have 4,500 deaths a year reported to me and they are all suspect deaths. I also supervise the entire service for five million people."

"And so you are telling us that ... that you supervise the deaths of all the people in the state of Massachusetts?"

"No. They are not all dead yet."

This time there were a few muffled laughs among the spectators and a couple of the jurors even chuckled. The audience was finding Dr. Ford quite entertaining. Anjette sneezed and blew her nose.

The attorney then asked about the use of arsenic for medical purposes.

"Arsenic is no longer used as a medicine in modern society."

"You say it is not any more being used ... up in Massachusetts?" Buffington asked.

"Not in Georgia either," Ford said pointedly.

"Have you discussed that matter with some of these south Georgia doctors?"

"No, but I know a lot of Georgians who have been classmates of mine in Boston. I know that Georgia medicine is excellent."

That point clearly went to Ford.

At the morning break, the Massachusetts doctor was the main topic of conversation among the spectators.

"He sure did know what he was talking about," a middle-aged woman declared.

"And he's so funny," her companion said. "I love the way he talks — like Cary Grant or somebody."

When Investigator Ray Stewart of the Bibb County Sheriff's Office was called next, he spent several minutes telling the court about the execution of the search warrant at Anjette's home. Hank O'Neal then handed him two pieces of onionskin paper that he asked the witness to identify. One appeared to be a partial draft of Julia Lyles's letter of apology — the mention of which had tantalized the court watchers for days. The other paper had only Julia Lyles's name on it, written over and over.

"I found those in this Whitman candy box under a dressing table in Anjette Lyles's bedroom."

O'Neal retrieved yet another piece of paper from his table. "Now, Mr. Witness, where was this paper found?"

"In a cloth handbag in the small closet in her bedroom."

O'Neal held it up for all to see. "Now, listen and see if this is the identical document which you found. It reads: 'Georgia, Bibb County. To Whom it May Concern: In the event of my death my daughter-in-law, Anjette Donovan Lyles, is to have charge of all funeral arrangements as I have discussed such arrangements with her and she knows my wishes and desires concerning the same. Memorial Chapel is to take charge of my body and is to handle the funeral. This 2nd day of September 1957.' With the name Julia Young Lyles appearing on the paper. The paper further appearing to have been witnessed by three persons. Is that the paper you found there that day?"

"That's it."

"Now what did you do with these papers?"

"Brought them to the Sheriff's office for transmission to the State Crime Lab."

O'Neal asked about the finding of a pad of paper under Anjette's bed, but the courtroom's attention had shifted from the witness to the defense table where Anjette was leaning back in her chair to speak to Chief Deputy Billy Murphy.

"I feel awful," she whispered. "Can we take a break? I've got to get some aspirin or something."

Murphy quietly approached the bench and whispered to the judge, who interrupted the proceedings. "Ladies and gentlemen, we will take a fifteen minute recess."

The jurors and the defendant were escorted out of the courtroom, but few spectators left their chairs, not wanting to risk losing their hard won seats. The recess stretched to over an hour. In her cell, Anjette waited until the county physician, Dr. W. E. Pound, arrived. He checked her over, asked about her symptoms, and reached a quick diagnosis—a head cold. He prescribed aspirin, liquids and rest.

By 3:00 P.M., the Yankees were within minutes of winning the seventh and last World Series game, but none of the players in the legal drama unfolding in Macon gave a passing thought to the events taking place several hundred miles away.

Anjette returned to the courtroom and people noticed she now had a blue sweater draped around her shoulders. She took her seat and opened her Bible, not even looking up when Investigator Stewart returned to the stand.

William Buffington spent little time questioning Stewart about the papers he had been brought to the stand to identify. It was the other items found in Anjette's house that interested the defense attorney.

"What else was in this Whitman candy box?"

"Well, several other papers and some pictures, a roll of negatives and some stamps. And there was a little note—written on it was 'love recipe.'"

"Love recipe." Buffington repeated. He gave the jury a significant look. "What other items were found?"

"We found a few unburned candles in a sack—they were about a foot long, I would say. And several bottles containing fluid."

"What colors were those candles?"

Stewart shook his head. "I don't recall."

The investigator was clearly disinterested in candles and Buffington excused him.

Nora Bagley, a country woman from Cochran, Georgia, was called to testify. She sat on the edge of the chair and answered the prosecutor's questions in a clear voice.

After establishing that she was familiar with her sister Julia's handwriting, O'Neal gave her several pieces of paper to examine. As she verified that the writing was indeed Julia's, she described for the court what each paper was. Mention of such homey things as a recipe for chocolate cake and a page from her address book altered the perceptions of those in the courtroom. Julia Lyles evolved from a faceless victim to a real woman who baked cakes, wrote letters and shared recipes.

With the identity of the handwriting established to his satisfaction, O'Neal moved the witness to the last days of her sister's life. Bagley recalled visiting Julia the day before her death and testified that her sister gave her $2,500 in post office certificates.

The second expert of the day came in an unlikely package. Where Dr. Ford's very appearance was solemn and scholarly, the sixty-eight-year-old Mary Beacom, document examiner for the State Crime Lab, resembled nothing more than somebody's sweet little grandmother.

She was a short, bespectacled woman wearing a plain brown suit with a cloche hat jammed down on her head.

Anjette still wasn't feeling well. She sat with her head resting in her hand. She barely glanced at the woman taking the stand.

Beginning her career as a teacher in Minnesota, Beacom had worked for many years as a document examiner in the private sector before being hired by the Georgia State Crime Lab in 1953. She had no trouble commanding the attention of the court. She testified, she had examined a number of papers found in Anjette Lyles's house, along with the burial instruction document and Julia Lyles's will and had compared them to known samples of the dead woman's handwriting. She had also compared the letter inquiring about his insurance to known samples of Buddy Gabbert's writing.

William Buffington objected when Julia's will was mentioned. "Your honor, that will has already been probated. The prosecution is making an unjustified attack on that document."

O'Neal assured the court he wasn't attacking the will. "I am only attempting to show that the signature on it was a forgery and thereby establish a motive for murder."

On that fine, if not to say nearly indistinguishable, point of law, the judge agreed with the prosecution and allowed the testimony.

To illustrate her findings, Mrs. Beacom had brought photographic blowups of the documents in question which she displayed on several easels at the front of the room where she could walk from one to another, using a pointer to indicate particular points. The same enlargements, on a smaller scale, had been reproduced in booklets and were distributed to the jurors.

Sounding more like a housewife explaining the intricacies of a favorite recipe than a scientist, the motherly little woman pointed to particular aspects of each enlargement indicating lines and loops and pen strokes. She paced back and forth in front of the jury box explaining how she recognized forgeries. In a manner reminiscent of her former occupation, she occasionally took note of a juror who looked lost or confused. Stopping her explanation, she'd walk over and show him the correct page in his book, then resume her testimony. Both the prosecution and defense attorneys left their tables and moved to the front of the courtroom for a better look.

Mary Beacom unequivocally declared that the signature on the insurance letter was not Gabbert's. She was equally positive that the signatures on Julia Lyles's will and on the burial instructions were forgeries.

"They were definitely traced."

Tracing, she explained, produced writing made up of many tentative strokes rather than the flowing lines seen in normal handwriting.

"As soon as I saw these signatures, I was suspicious."

Through a number of scientific tests, she was able to bear out that suspicion. "Many over-writings, tracings, and indentions around the signatures."

Finally, to the delight of her audience, she gave an impromptu lesson in forgery. Her finale was to have Hank O'Neal write his name and then produce a passable forgery of his signature. She did so, explaining every one of her actions to the court as she went.

O'Neal displayed her finished work to the jury, good-naturedly calling what she had done a "little crime".

It was nearly 6:00 P.M. when Mary Beacom finished her direct testimony and Judge Long called it a day.

Thursday night was a low point for Anjette. She still felt stuffy and feverish, and her usually hearty appetite dulled. Byrice Goings checked on her several times during the evening, feeling her forehead for signs of fever and making sure she took the medicine Dr. Pound had recommended. The jailer's wife tried to cheer her up, but Anjette remained unresponsive. Whether it was the effects of the cold or the realization that the trial was not going well for her, she was unusually pessimistic. It seemed to Byrice that Anjette was seriously considering for the first time the possibility that she might be found guilty.

CHAPTER FOURTEEN

JUST BEFORE 9:00 A.M. ON FRIDAY MORNING, JETTA AND ALICE Donovan pushed through the mob of people outside the courthouse and up the front steps. Photographers scurried after them and reporters surged forward, shouting their names and hoping for a useable quote. Blythe McKay from the *Macon Telegraph* was one of those asking about Anjette's health. Jetta surprised her by stopping to answer her question.

"Well, she had a sore throat the day before yesterday," the older woman said, echoing every mother who has ever been concerned about a sick child. "Then it developed into a cold. And she was nauseated yesterday. The strain of the trial probably has something to do with it. My daddy was like that. If he got upset about something, he went to bed."

As the two women continued their progress up the steps, several photographers jumped forward again and Jetta dodged behind McKay.

"There they are again," she complained angrily. "Can't you do anything about them making so many pictures of us? *We* haven't done anything."

Anjette had dressed in a dark wool skirt and a light blue sweater set, anticipating a return of yesterday's chill, but her head was clearer this morning and the aspirin had taken care of the fever. She walked into the courtroom with her head held habitually high, sat down and opened her Bible.

When all the seats were filled and Judge Long was on the bench, Mary Beacom returned to the witness stand for cross examination. She was as cheerful and irrepressible as ever. When Buffington asked if there were methods of forgery other than those she had demonstrated the day before, she beamed as if a favorite student had asked a particularly insightful question.

"I gave several, but I didn't exhaust the methods of forgery! They go as far back as Jezebel and the Book of Kings."

He didn't ask for any elaboration on that theme, but more then one spectator pulled out her Bible that evening to learn just what Jezebel did in the way of forgery.

Cross-examining Beacom was nearly a waste of time and Buffington knew it. There was no chance he would shake her conclusions about the validity of the signatures in question. Even trying to do so could be a serious error. The little handwriting expert had become so popular with the jury that any attack on her would most likely backfire. He settled for having her admit that, even though the signatures were forgeries, she could not say for sure who had forged them. Then he excused her from any further questioning.

Wyolene Poole, business manager at Parkview Hospital, followed Mary Beacom. She was clearly embarrassed to have to admit that, even though she had notarized Julia Lyles's signature on the burial arrangement as Anjette had asked her to, she had not actually seen the older woman sign it.

"Mrs. Anjette Lyles came to my office and stated that Mrs. Lyles had just signed this paper and asked if I would notarize it."

"What did you say or do?" O'Neal asked.

"I typed in the date and, assuming that the statements made by Anjette Lyles were correct, I accommodated her and notarized it."

She went on to explain that her sister, Evelyn Nutt, also was present and had signed the document as a witness.

"Julia *did* write out that burial arrangement," Anjette whispered to Buffington. "I don't care what anyone says. She *did.*"

Jetta reached over to give her daughter's arm a reassuring pat.

Unable to successfully challenge the handwriting expert, Buffington jumped into the cross-examination of Wyolene Poole with both feet. It was a one-sided battle.

"I'll ask you then, Mrs. Poole, why you bothered to type down there that your sister was the second witness. The document already purports to have one witness, does it not?"

"I was working on the assumption that the statement given me by Anjette Lyles was correct," she said defensively.

"Yes, ma'am. But that is not an answer to my question. I asked why you put underneath that typing 'second witness, E. Nutt.' First witness was Mrs. J. B. Bryan, wasn't it?"

"That was the signature on there, yes."

"So why did you go to the trouble to put down there 'second witness' if she was in fact witnessing your signature?"

Poole frowned, trying to understand what he wanted. She tried again. "Because according to the assumption I have just given you, I assumed that Mrs. Anjette Lyles was giving me the correct information."

"Now, Mrs. Poole, that is not at all in response to my question. I asked you why you put 'second witness' down there. Why didn't you just put down 'E. Nutt'?"

"I can't explain any more than I have." Her breathing had accelerated. "You can ask me any other questions that would enlighten me. I'll be glad to ..."

"All right, Mrs. Poole," he interrupted. "How long ... Since when ... How long you been a notary public?"

"Since about 1943."

He nodded. "Well, now, Mrs. Poole, when else during the course of your exercising the prerogative that has been granted to you by the state of Georgia to be a notary public have you ever seen it necessary to get somebody to witness your signature as a notary? Can you answer that?"

"The usual forms, court forms, have more than one witness."

"And that is the only explanation you could give to the court and jury?"

"The only explanation I have to offer, yes."

He moved on. "Do you have with you, Mrs. Poole, the instruction book sent to you by the Secretary of State?" he asked, referring to the booklet handed out with every notary public commission.

"I ... believe it is at my home."

"Did you comply with the provision of laws of the state of Georgia?"

She shook her head miserably. "In not witnessing the signature, I did not."

Everyone in the courtroom, with the possible exception of the defense team, was relieved when the poor woman was allowed to leave the stand. All Buffington had proven was that he could confuse a frightened woman who had been forced to admit in public that she had failed to perform her duty correctly. No one believed she had intended to do wrong. She had just tried to help someone else and no one in that courtroom had enjoyed watching her discomfort. The defense gained nothing in the exchange and the stories that appeared in Saturday's newspapers painted Poole as an overworked woman whose only mistake was trusting Anjette Lyles.

Julia's niece, Katharine Gurr, testified next. Anjette regarded her cousin with no expression at all.

Katharine didn't meet the defendant's eyes. She and Anjette should have been closer. Her own son, Roger, had been born on the same day as Marcia. But Anjette wasn't an easy person to feel close to, and on this early October Friday, her purpose in the courtroom was not to support her cousin. She was there to help establish the other woman's guilt.

O'Neal used Gurr's testimony to emphasize the fact that Julia Lyles had been unable to use her hands during her last illness.

"She couldn't hold a glass and she couldn't hold a straw to drink water out of," Gurr said. "I held the glass for her."

"What was the matter with her hands?"

"They were so swollen, she had no use of them."

Katharine's mother, Nettie Young, and her aunt, Pansy Hall, followed her on the stand to confirm her testimony.

"Her hands were just swollen till they looked ready to burst," Young told the court.

O'Neal wrapped up this line of questioning with Pansy Hall. "Of all your visits to her in the hospital, did you see your sister successfully do any solitary thing with her hands?"

"No. Never."

Then the prosecution introduced a long list of medical witnesses. Margaret Parker, Avis Connell and Mildred Thompson were each on the witness stand only a short time—just long enough to describe Julia Lyles's condition during her last hospitalization. They were all in agreement that, from the day she was admitted, the woman had been unable to use her hands for even the simplest tasks. However, Jennie Ingle's testimony stretched to over an hour. In a soft, almost shy voice, the nurse told how she had cared for Buddy Gabbert, Julia Lyles and Marcia Lyles. For once, Anjette paid close attention to what was being said about her.

Ingle's description of Buddy Gabbert's suffering was graphic, making his agony real for everyone in the courtroom. This testimony was especially wrenching for his relatives. At one point, D. K. Gabbert covered his eyes with his hand, as if by doing so he might be able to avoid picturing his brother's pain.

"It was the awfulest thing I've ever seen in the way of a rash," Ingle said. "It was running, oozing, weeping in a lot of places, even from his ears and everywhere."

Shocked whispers followed her account of meeting Anjette on the street only weeks after Gabbert's death and being told about the new boyfriend—who also happened to be Buddy's boss.

"She told me how much money he made and that he had a big insurance policy and that he was very kind and sweet to her. She said, 'I'm flying high. I'm feeling no pain.'"

The courtroom mood didn't soften when Ingle repeated an earlier conversation she'd had with Anjette concerning Julia Lyles.

"I was having lunch at the restaurant with Anjette when Mrs. Lyles, Mrs. Julia Lyles, came in from the kitchen. I said, 'Oh, there's Mrs. Lyles.'"

"What did the defendant say?"

"She said, 'The old devil! I hate her. I wish she was dead.' That's exactly what she said."

Several times as Jennie testified Anjette slowly shook her head as if unable to believe what she was hearing.

Testimony continued with the nurse telling the court that Anjette had asked several times if Buddy, and later Julia, were going to die. When Jennie described little Marcia Lyles's condition shortly before the child's death, her voice choked with tears.

"She was in an oxygen tent. She looked swollen, bleeding at the mouth and nose and kind of fretful at intervals."

Lehman Myers, the car dealer from whom Anjette purchased the white Cadillac three months after Buddy's death, took the stand next to relate how that sale had come about.

"Did she trade in her old car?" Charles Adams asked.

"Yes, sir, a '55 Oldsmobile."

"How was the difference in price handled?"

"She gave a check for the difference. A check for $2,538.50."

It was a fortunate there were no major medical emergencies in Macon that afternoon, because it seemed that most of the Parkview Hospital nursing staff had been summoned to the Bibb County Courthouse.

Hazel Shea was called as the next witness. Once again, the prosecution asked one of its witnesses to describe Buddy Gabbert's condition during his time in Parkview Hospital.

"He was in intense pain, almost without relief at any time. Continuously—day and night."

O'Neal gave Anjette a look, then asked, "Did you ever see the defendant show any emotion of any kind over the condition of her husband?"

Shea shook her head. "She seemed disinterested most of the time."

Nurse Rubye Lines took Hazel's place on the stand. She described Julia Lyles's last stay in the hospital.

"Did Anjette Lyles have anything to say to you about any bonds?" O'Neal asked with an abrupt change of subject.

"Yes. She was upset—very upset—because the bonds had been removed the day before. She said they should not have been removed from the purse."

"Was Anjette Lyles present when Mrs. Ben Lyles died?"

"Yes, she was."

"What was she doing immediately prior to Mrs. Ben Lyles's death?"

Lines shrugged. "Well, she'd go out frequently and make phone calls. And she would ask me how much longer it would be before the patient died."

"Did she ask that repeatedly?"

"Yes, she did."

O'Neal took a deep breath. "Now tell the jury, immediately after Mrs. Lyles died, did you see any reaction such as grief or sorrow in this defendant?"

"Not right afterwards—when it was just she and I—no. Not until several people were present."

"When those people showed up, what did she do?"

"She cried."

Leila Radlein, who attended Marcia during the last days of her life, took the stand. She had just described the child's hallucinations—"She saw snakes. She thought she had bugs crawling out of her fingers—" when she was suddenly interrupted by a din of drums, cymbals and brass that rose from the street where a local high school band led a homecoming parade. For a few frustrating moments, Hank O'Neal tried to continue, once even cupping his hands around his mouth and shouting to try and make himself heard, but it was useless. He finally raised his hands in a gesture of surrender.

"Your honor, I give up."

So the most sensational trial ever held in Macon was suspended for a few minutes while children in bright uniforms played shiny instruments and made their way down Mulberry Street in one of the classic rites of autumn.

Once the parade moved on and order was restored, Radlein went on with her testimony. She didn't try to hide her anger when she recounted Anjette's reaction to Marcia's hallucination-induced terror.

"She acted as though it was very comical. She laughed."

O'Neal made sure this accusation was heard by everyone. "She did what?" he asked disbelievingly.

"She laughed."

As the afternoon progressed, more nurses took the stand. Jacqueline Sirany and Emogene Dobbs both confirmed Radlein's testimony that Anjette had laughed at Marcia's reaction to the imagined horrors.

Anjette felt Buffington's eyes on her. She turned and met his stare. He was the one who looked away first.

Emogene Dobbs had tended Marcia Lyles for three nights—March 19, 20 and 21—and described what had happened the second shift she worked.

"It was about 11:30 that night and Mrs. Lyles told me Marcia would be dead by 2:00 A.M."

"What did she do after making that statement?"

"Well, a lot of things had been collected in the room over the period of Marcia's illness. She had a lot of books and flowers and clothes and personal things. Mrs. Lyles packed them all up and put them in suitcases. She picked up Marcia's socks and said, 'Well, she won't be using these anymore.' She discarded all the flowers and put the suitcases out in the hall. She kept some of the flower vases and said she was going to take them to the cemetery."

"Did Marcia die that night?"

"No, sir. She didn't die until the night of April fifth."

Natalie Wilson, who'd been assigned to Marcia's case for twenty of the days she was hospitalized, also testified that Anjette laughed at Marcia's terror during her hallucinations. Wilson also had been present when the little girl died.

"Was she conscious?" O'Neal asked.

"She seemed to be. She would open her eyes and would talk to us, but she was very weak."

"Now, immediately after Marcia's death, did anybody commence crying?"

"Yes, some of the family. Mrs. Donovan was there and Anjette's sister-in-law."

"Did Anjette Lyles make any statement directed toward any person that was crying?"

"Yes, she said she didn't want any crying and she wished they would go on out. She didn't want to see anybody crying."

That ended Wilson's direct testimony and it was Roy Rhodenhiser, not Buffington, who got to his feet. After a few preliminary questions, he turned his attention to Anjette's behavior during Marcia's hallucinations.

"Now, Mrs. Wilson, you stated a moment ago that Mrs. Lyles would laugh when the child was seeing these bugs and snakes and bees. What did you do?"

"Well, it shocked me so. I ... She noticed that I looked at her kind of funny, I'm sure."

"Well, isn't it customary, Mrs. Wilson, to try to cheer up someone and reassure them when they have these hallucinations such as you have described?"

Wilson looked dubious at the phrase "cheer up", but nodded agreement.

"So it was nothing unusual about a mother trying to cheer up a child?"

"It didn't seem to me that was what she was trying to do."

"Well, now, will you describe that to us please, ma'am, the difference between trying to cheer her up and what she was trying to do?"

There was an edge of sarcasm in the attorney's voice, but Natalie Wilson ignored it. "She didn't talk directly to Marcia and try to reassure her about the insects not being there. She was just laughing at her."

Rhodenhiser was reluctant to give up. "From your observation as a nurse, which is better on the patient: for the people in the room to act terrified or to act calm and try to cheer them up?"

"Well, certainly not to act terrified. Just reassure them."

"Try and make them happy?"

"Yes."

When the defense had finished with Wilson, O'Neal stood for redirect. He approached the stand and smiled at the witness.

"Now, Mr. Rhodenhiser asked you something of the best methods for handling a patient who was undergoing the type of agony which you have described. Is it your opinion that to stand back and laugh at a person would be of any help?"

Wilson shot a look of vindication at Rhodenhiser, then answered, "No, it would not."

She left the stand, apparently still angry at Rhodenhiser's questions, and O'Neal called Rosemary Reynolds to testify.

Rosemary hadn't seen Anjette since May, and was shocked by the changes in her appearance. The weight gain was sad for a woman who'd always worked so hard to keep her figure. And Rosemary could see the strain in her face and the dark circles beneath her eyes. Her heart went out to her friend.

She raised her right hand and swore to tell the truth and Hank O'Neal asked her to think back to the time Julia Lyles had been hospitalized. "Tell the jury what was the first thing that you ever saw Anjette Lyles fix to take to her?"

"Some buttermilk. She poured it in a glass about half full."

"Then what did she do?"

"She got her bag and taken the half glass of buttermilk in the bathroom."

"How long did she stay in there?"

"Oh, it wasn't but a few minutes. Then she left the bathroom and went out the back door to the hospital. She said she was taking it to Mrs. Lyles because it was the only thing that would stay on her stomach."

Rosemary testified she had seen Anjette go through this same routine on two more occasions while Julia was sick.

Before she left the stand, O'Neal had her describe how Anjette had made lemonade for her hospitalized daughter. Rosemary hated telling all these things—she knew they hurt Anjette—but she also knew she had to tell the truth. She just hoped that, when Anjette got the chance to talk to the jury, everything could be explained.

Judge Long recessed the court at 7:00 P.M. The jurors, who had been sitting in the hard, straight-backed chairs since early that morning, got stiffly to their feet. They had been sequestered now for five days and were feeling very much like prisoners themselves. None of them looked forward to another night in the dormitory.

Out on the sidewalk in front of the courthouse, a reporter from an Atlanta newspaper approached Jetta and Alice. "How can you sit there, day after day, knowing what Anjette is charged with?" she asked.

Jetta turned to her, her face twisted by anger and pain. "Listen, I don't care if she's killed everybody in Macon or if she hasn't killed anybody. That's my *daughter* in there. What do you expect a mother to do?"

They hurried away before more questions could be asked.

CHAPTER FIFTEEN

OCTOBER ELEVENTH WAS A GOLDEN DAY. THE SEASON HAD changed overnight and the sky, glimpsed through the branches of towering dark green pines, was that heartbreaking shade of blue seen only in autumn. Cool, dry and sunny, Saturday was an ideal day to rake leaves, romp with a dog, go to a county fair or cheer for a favorite football team. Southerners take their football very seriously, and that day the state's two major college teams each played arch rivals. Georgia Tech took on Tennessee while the University of Georgia was pitted against Florida State. If they weren't in attendance at one of the big stadiums, most Georgians were home listening to one of the games on radio. But in Bibb County Superior Court, Saturday was just another day of the week. Anjette Lyles's trial continued in the old brick courthouse; Judge Long was not about to suspend the proceedings just because it was the weekend. Court started promptly at 9:00 A.M.

There were more male faces in the audience that morning than there had been during the week. A few college girls, giggling to cover their nervousness, crowded onto the benches and, here and there, mothers held small children on their laps, shushing them anxiously to keep them quiet. No one doubted that Judge Long expected silence.

Anjette's attorneys told her that the prosecution was nearing the end of its presentation. As witnesses were called, she realized they were finishing their case with her own employees. While the waitresses and cooks were unanimous in their affection for little Marcia Lyles, none even hinted at a fondness for Anjette. And, unlike Rosemary Reynolds, they weren't reluctant to testify. They all told of Anjette's cursing and threatening Marcia and described the food and drink she'd prepared and, after taking it behind closed doors, carried to the victims in the hospital.

O'Neal questioned Cleo Hutchinson about the night Marcia became ill at the restaurant. "Did she ask the defendant to take her home?"

"Yes."

"What did the defendant say?"

"Well, she was in the kitchen with a whole bunch of her friends. She told her to shut up and leave her alone."

When Jack Gautier confronted Cleo, he suggested that Marcia had spent the day in question with someone other than her mother. Hadn't Marcia arrived at the restaurant with Lewis Watkins, Anjette's uncle? he asked.

"No." Cleo was sure. "She did not come in with nobody but Anjette Lyles."

"Wasn't anybody else with her?"

"Nobody else with her but Anjette Lyles. And Carla."

The next witness, Fannie Butts, didn't try to hide the fact that she loved Marcia. Tears filled her eyes when the subject of the child's death was brought up. Once or twice, she had to stop speaking until she could get her voice under control. She told the jury how, after Julia Lyles's death, Anjette's treatment of her daughter changed. Her description of Anjette shaking and threatening the little girl was a sad repetition of testimony already given by others.

"She called Marcia a 'little Lyles-looking S. B.,'" Fannie said.

Hank O'Neal understood her reluctance, but he knew the jury needed to hear the actual words.

"Well, now, 'course you are in court," he told her gently, "but you can say it. We are going to ask you now to say just what she said. Tell the jury what she said without any of that S. B. business."

Fannie tried evasion. "Said she was going to kill the little so and so if it was the last thing she ever do."

O'Neal shook his head. "Tell us what it was. I know you don't want to say."

He was right, of course. Fannie Butts—a good Christian woman—didn't want to say the words. But she took a deep breath and forced herself to do what had to be done. "Well, she said, 'I'm going to kill the little Lyles-looking son of a bitch if it is the last thing I ever do.'"

Fannie cried, dabbing at her eyes with a flowered handkerchief, when she related how Anjette had told her that Marcia knew she was going to die. "She told me that Marcy said she was going home to be with Little Lyles."

"Who was this Little Lyles?"

"...Her grandmother." At that, the witness began sobbing. There was considerable sniffling and throat-clearing in the room as the spectators reacted to the testimony. A deputy who had been standing at the back of the courtroom slipped out into the corridor to regain control of himself. Anjette didn't cry. She remained still and expressionless as people around her wept for her dead daughter.

Next on the stand was Willa Mae Davis. She, too, had seen Anjette prepare lemonade for Marcia. She said that Carrie Jackson had motioned for her to watch, so she was paying particular attention when Anjette picked up the juice and took it, along with her purse, into the restroom. When she returned to the kitchen, Anjette stirred the drink, then put the spoon to her lips.

O'Neal pursued that. "All right, now, you stated this defendant touched that stuff to her mouth?"

"Yes, sir."

"Now tell this jury whether or not following that you had any opportunity to observe the defendant's mouth?"

"Yes, sir," Davis said. "Approximately two days later, she came down to the restaurant and it was broke out in sores."

Davis testified to hearing Anjette predict her daughter's death on more than one occasion and told of a night, weeks before Marcia died, when Anjette decided death was imminent. She began clearing out the hospital room and giving away the child's possessions.

Alice Donovan, sitting at the defense table, cried softly during that part of the testimony.

Of all the restaurant employees, Carrie Jackson had been the closest to the Lyles family, having begun working for them as a girl of seventeen. Marcia, the first grandchild, had been her particular favorite.

"How long you known Marcia?" O'Neal asked.

"I knowed Marcy from the time she was born until the time she died."

"What was your feelings toward Marcia?"

"I loved Marcy," she said, tears welling in her eyes.

Carrie told of Anjette's strange behavior when preparing food and drink for Julia Lyles during her last illness, then seeing the process repeated when Marcia was in the hospital.

"Did you yourself do any act on behalf of Marcia Lyles?"

"Yes, sir," she said with no hesitation, "I did. I wrote a letter, that's what I did."

With that one sentence, Jackson cleared up a mystery that had tormented the town for months. At last it was known who authored the anonymous letters that started the investigation.

O'Neal wasn't interested in exploring the specific allegations in the letters. "You need not tell us what was in it; that's not necessary. But who did you write it to?"

"Mrs. Bagley."

"Did you sign your name to it?"

"No, I didn't."

On cross-examination, Gautier returned to a topic that was fast becoming a favorite of the defense—voodoo and its accouterments. O'Neal objected, concerned they were trying to lay a foundation for an insanity defense, but Gautier contended that his motive for the questions was simple. He wanted to show the jury the kind of person who believed in magic and would make predictions about her relatives based on that belief. Long allowed him to continue.

"Who burned those candles?"

"*She* burnt them," Jackson said, as if reluctant to speak Anjette's name.

"Who is 'she'?"

"Miss Anjette."

"Did you talk to Mrs. Lyles about burning these candles?"

"No, sir," the cook said, making it clear she wasn't interested in candles or spells or anything else of that nature. "I didn't talk to her about them."

"She never told you what they meant?"

She shrugged. "It wasn't my business what she was burning them for."

He went on to quiz her about roots, potions, powders and love recipes, but Carrie stolidly maintained she had never seen anything like that around the restaurant. Her listeners were left with the impression that she wouldn't have deigned to notice them if they had been there.

After lunch, Leonard Campbell, the county medical examiner, was recalled to testify about a conversation he'd had with the defendant the week after Marcia's death. He had, he explained to the court, told Anjette that he had heard rumors that Marcia had been poisoned, and that some people were even saying that she had poisoned the child.

"What was her reaction?"

"There was none."

But, he went on, Anjette had called him the next day and said she had to see him. Although it was after 5:00 P.M. and his nurse had left for the day, he agreed, and Anjette and Carla arrived in his office a short time later. Anjette had prodded Carla until she recited, in a childish monotone that she had been playing with the ant poison. As if to verify it, Anjette handed him a brown paper bag containing two partially full bottles of Terro ant poison, and advised that when this occurred, Carla had been playing with the Jones twins. Campbell related that he examined Carla, and when he found her in good health, asked her mother if the Jones twins were all right. In answer to his concerned question, she admitted she hadn't mentioned it to their mother. Campbell demanded she do so immediately.

He described Anjette's looking up the number in the telephone book and placing the call. The conversation had been brief—Anjette identified herself, recounted what she had told Campbell about the children playing with poison, and hung up.

"Can you tell this jury," O'Neal asked, "with reference to that conversation, what was the first thing that she said?"

"She said that this was Anjette Lyles and she was in Dr. Campbell's office."

Carmen Howard had worked as a maid and housekeeper for Anjette Lyles since 1953. She was called to the stand early Saturday afternoon and stated that she, too, had seen Anjette preparing lemonade for Marcia and had heard the death predictions. It was Carmen, the jury learned, who had first found bottles of ant poison in the Pinewood Drive house—in Anjette's purse and, on the day of Marcia's funeral, in her dresser drawer. Carmen also described seeing Anjette desperately searching her own house a week or so after Marcia's funeral.

"During that morning, she tote out everything in the house," Carmen told the court. "Said she was looking for a letter."

According to Carmen, her employer hadn't found the letter that day, but was successful the next.

"She told me that she had find the letter, said she find it lying in Mrs. Lyles's old pocketbook."

"And what did she say about the letter?"

"She said it's something that might come up, and the letter would clear her."

"Did she tell you to do anything about the letter?"

Carmen nodded. "Yes, sir. She told me if anybody ask about the letter to tell them that I find the letter."

O'Neal looked over his shoulder to be sure the jurors were paying attention. "On the Tuesday after Marcia's funeral, did you receive a telephone call from Mrs. Anjette Lyles?"

"Yes, sir. She called me about six o'clock in the afternoon."

"Tell this jury when you picked up that phone and the defendant started talking to you, where did she tell you she was calling from?"

"She said she was calling from Dr. Campbell's office. She said the twins and Carla were playing doctor and they were playing with some Terro ant poison bottles. She said Carla found them in the lower cabinet in the bathroom and she was afraid that Carla had drink some. She had taken Carla down to Dr. Campbell to be examined."

Mrs. Charles Jones, an attractive, understated young woman, was the next witness. O'Neal established that she lived near the Lyles home and that she was the mother of twin girls who sometimes played with Carla and Marcia. The twins and Carla attended the same kindergarten and often rode to and from school together. She said the last time they had played together was in April when Carmen Howard had picked up all three girls after school and driven them back to the Pinewood Drive house.

"Would you tell this jury whether or not you had a telephone number listed in the Bibb County directory at that time."

"No, sir, I did not."

"Following that visit—your children with Carla Lyles—did you ever, at any time, receive a telephone call from Anjette Donovan Lyles with reference to your children playing with arsenic poison?"

"No, I did not."

"If you had ever received any such call, would you have remembered it?"

"I certainly would!" she declared.

Funeral director Joe Southerland was called next and told the court that Anjette had ordered a casket for Marcia some two weeks before her death—at about the same time the doctors were telling her the child appeared to be recovering.

When the prosecution called Robert Hunter, many spectators were puzzled. The witness's name was not familiar and many didn't recognize the man who took the stand.

The five days of testimony had been sprinkled with references to witnesses' conversations with Anjette about her need to purchase or keep Terro ant poison. It had been reported that she'd complained of problems with ants—both at her home and at the restaurant. Robert Hunter was an employee of a local pest control company. That company had maintained a contract for the restaurant and the Pinewood Drive house for two years. He himself had provided the service on that contract since 1957, spraying both locations every month. There had never, he declared, been a problem with ants in either location. If there had been, he assured the court, his company would have taken care of it immediately. The company did not charge for additional visits.

William Buffington's cross examination of the witness provided a gentle break in the tension of the trial. "Did I understand you to say that ants are easy to control?"

"Yes, sir," Hunter said with the confidence of a professional. "For me it's easy to control ants."

"It's easy for you to control them?"

"That's right. I have very little trouble with ants."

Buffington grinned. "Well, would you give me a call after this case is over?"

"I sure will. Be glad to. What's your number?"

Even Judge Long smiled at that.

The prosecution's last witness was Harry L. Harris. As lead investigator, he had spent the trial at the prosecution table and, on this Saturday afternoon, he was fighting to stay awake. His first child, a son, had been born the night before and he hadn't slept for nearly forty-eight hours.

O'Neal began by asking about his interview of the defendant on the day she'd been booked into the Bibb County Jail.

"When you first asked whether she had benefited from each of these people, what did she say?"

"She said she hadn't," Harris said. "I told her we would check, and if she wasn't telling the truth, we'd know."

O'Neal nodded. "And did she then volunteer any information?"

"She said yes, she had, and she could save us the trouble."

He related how Anjette had then listed the insurance policies and the will from which she benefited. From the notes he'd taken of that interview, Harris calculated that Anjette's financial rewards amounted to just under $50,000.

Adams and O'Neal had spent months planning each step of their case. They thought they knew exactly what was needed to convince a jury of Anjette Lyles's guilt. As each point was made—opportunity, motive, one incriminating fact after another—they marked it off the checklist. Every night that week, they had reviewed the day's events and discussed what they wanted from the next day's witnesses. They had presented fifty-one witnesses. Now that Harry Harris's testimony was in the record, the last piece of the puzzle had been eased into place. They believed the jury had everything they needed for a conviction. Looking as weary as he felt, O'Neal stood and faced the judge.

"Your honor, the prosecution rests."

It was 6:00 P.M. and Judge Long recessed for the day. The trial would reconvene at 9:00 A.M. Monday morning, giving most everyone a welcome day off. However, the jurors—and the defendant, of course—got no respite. The thirteen men returned to the dormitory they were beginning to hate, with nothing more to look forward to than another twenty-four hours of captivity.

CHAPTER SIXTEEN

MOST PEOPLE EXPECTED MONDAY TO BE THE LAST DAY OF THE trial. There was furious speculation as to how the defense would counter the damaging testimony that had been presented over the past five days. Who were their witnesses? How would they defend what had been said? And most intriguing of all, would Anjette take the stand?

But the court watchers were in for a surprise. The anticipated parade of witnesses never materialized. Buffington and his colleagues put up no evidence. Anjette Lyles was their only show. In 1958, Georgia law provided for defendants in capital cases to make only unsworn statements, and cross examination was forbidden.

Looking solemn and sincere, several pages of notes in one hand, Anjette made her way to the witness stand. She wore a long-sleeved black jersey dress with a big gold buckle. The famous platinum hair was demurely pinned up close to her head. She settled in the chair, turned slightly to her right so that she could face the jury and began to speak in a clear, calm voice.

"Gentlemen of the jury, I have not killed anyone," she began. "I want to tell you the truth about this."

Starting with her marriage to Ben Lyles in 1947, Anjette told them her life story—from her own perspective. She described her troubles with Ben, his drinking and his refusal to work. "But I loved him and I stayed with him, even though my family at times tried to get me to leave him."

She dismissed the idea that she received a significant financial gain from his death. "At the time, I didn't know how much insurance Little Ben had, but come to find out he had $3,000 worth of insurance. That was not much money for a widow with two children, specially babies and one of them a sickly child."

She told of meeting Buddy Gabbert, their marriage and his final illness, explaining with a sad smile why she had objected to his autopsy. "One night we were all discussing dying and somebody made mention about an autopsy. He said if he ever died, he did not want to be cut on and made me promise not to have him have an autopsy. I agreed to it and I told him if I died, I certainly didn't want an autopsy and he promised me I wouldn't have one."

She had kept careful track of the testimony against her and referred to her notes as she attempted to refute it, point by point.

Anjette told the jury that Buddy *should* have been in the hospital earlier, just as Jennie Ingle had said, but he had been such a difficult patient during his time at Parkview that his doctor couldn't get him into a Macon hospital. She described Buddy's illness and contradicted D. K. Gabbert, declaring that she had called Buddy's parents several times while he was sick.

Jetta wept softly as her daughter spoke, and several times Alice Donovan sobbed audibly.

Anjette took pains to speak clearly and deliberately. She wanted these men to understand. She assured them that she was truly fond of Julia Lyles and had always gotten along well with her. When she spoke of the testimony that had come from Marcia's nurses, she didn't hide her anger.

"The nurses omitted telling the jury how I would pick that child up in my arms and talk with her and tell her that Mother was here."

She told them she was the only one able to cajole the little girl into taking fluids when no one else could.

"I did all in the world I could to help them. At the time, Marcia was heavy. She weighed about a hundred and twelve or fifteen pounds. She was fat. She was real solid. They would want to move her, change her bed, and I would help pick her up and move her because she wouldn't let the nurses do it."

The only reason she was frequently absent from the room, she said, was that the nurses—Leila Radlein in particular—believed they could do more with the child if her mother was not there.

For a long while, she spoke about magic, her belief in root doctors, voodoo, potions and candles, assuring the jury she had confidence in these things.

"That day that I was arrested," she said, "there were roots in my pocketbook—different kinds of roots for different things. There is certain roots you can put in your mouth when you talk to people and you can get people to do what you want them to do."

Anjette was relaxed now, leaning back in the chair. She told them about the power of garlic and sprinkling salt, and of roots that made your wishes come true. She blamed the root doctors and fortune tellers she frequented for the predictions of death she had made. Those were *their* predictions, she insisted. She had simply been repeating them.

Anjette stopped her monologue to take a sip of water and gather her thoughts. The next part would be the hardest. She knew that the opinion of many of those in the courtroom had turned against her after the nurses' descriptions of her laughter during Marcia's hallucinations. She had to address that issue if she hoped to win over the jury.

"I have a nervous habit," she said, leaning a few inches in the jury's direction. "I have a twitch in my side from nerves and I have a nervous habit of, when I get upset, I laugh. I can't help it. I have done it all my life. Instead of crying, I laugh. It's a bad habit, but I have always had it. I can't help myself."

Her eyes filled with tears as she wrapped up her remarks. "I have never called my child a son of a bitch. I never did that in my life. I loved Marcia. I did not kill my child. I have not given my child any poison. I have certainly not killed Ben. I certainly did not kill Mrs. Lyles. I certainly did not kill Buddy. I hope that you all will believe me when I say that because it is the truth."

As Anjette got to her feet and walked back toward the defense table, the clock in the courthouse tower four floors above their heads began striking the noon hour. Jetta put an arm around her, and for the first time since the trial had begun, Anjette cried.

The lunch recess was called and ten minutes later Anjette was back in her cell at the top of the courthouse. The tears that she had held back for so long had brought a curious release of tension. She found she was hungry and ate all of her jailhouse lunch of blackeyed peas, corn, slaw and cornbread.

The afternoon session started at 2:30 and was devoted to closing arguments and the judge's charge to the jury. By not presenting any evidence, the defense was assured of the initial opening statement, and after the prosecutors had had their say, the last word to the jury.

Jack Gautier began the summing up for the defense. In a steady, businesslike voice, he told the jury the case against Anjette Lyles was purely circumstantial, and that no motive had been established. Of the $1,750 Anjette was to have received from Marcia's insurance, $1,200 had been spent on the child's funeral. Surely that didn't indicate greed as a motive. And, he continued, there was no basis for believing she hated the child, as the prosecution suggested, since they were able to produce only two instances in which Anjette treated her daughter with anything but kindness. He reminded his listeners of the numerous witnesses who had attested to the fact that Anjette was generous, even indulgent, with her children.

Gautier declared he was amazed at the thought that his client could be the shrewd criminal the prosecution made her out to be. She'd heard rumors of her impending arrest days before it happened, he told them, yet this "archcriminal" never removed the bottles of ant poison from her home. In fact, she had taken two bottles of the stuff to Dr. Campbell herself. He declared that the state had not made its case, and returned to his chair.

Charles Adams began the prosecution's closing statement. His first target was the statement Anjette had made only that morning. He professed great admiration for her performance.

"Even after the testimony of fifty-one people for the state, Anjette can get up on the stand and almost impress you—if you listen to her. The evidence in this case shows she has fooled a lot of people. She believed she could get on the stand and put one of those roots in her mouth and people would believe her."

He was confident, he said, that this jury would not be fooled, and asked them to remember the evidence instead of her statement. She deserved to die and he asked the jury to return a verdict of guilty with no recommendation of mercy. Then he relinquished the floor to Hank O'Neal.

From the street below came the muffled sound of a hymn played on the chimes of a downtown bank. It was nothing out of the ordinary—it happened every afternoon at 5:00—but it lent a righteous, almost holy air to O'Neal's words.

The defendant should die for her crimes, he said, then brutally listed the fate of each victim, claiming that, before bringing on death, the poison given to them by Anjette Lyles had turned one man insane, transformed a second into a running sore and made one woman a helpless cripple. He declared that Marcia, whom he described as a baby, had died in agony. The trial was not just about the defendant. He wanted to make sure they remembered the four people who had been murdered.

"Buddy Gabbert was a young boy from Texas," he said, "a long way from home." He angrily condemned efforts of defense counsel to portray his parents as uncaring and claimed they were trying to drive a wedge between the victim and his mother.

The only love Marcia Lyles ever knew, he told them, came from the cooks at her mother's restaurant and, they in the end, were the only ones who had tried to save the life of this "unwanted child."

"Thank God for Carrie Jackson," he said. "Because of her, we have finally learned the truth."

When O'Neal returned to his seat, there was a moment of silence before William Buffington approached the jury. With O'Neal's words still ringing in the air, he gave a little smile and shook his head at the impassioned speech made by the prosecutor. His opening remarks were a gentle complaint about the prosecutor's "display of drama".

Anjette cried quietly into a handkerchief while he reminded the jurors that she had received only $3,000 in insurance benefits after the death of her first husband, surely not an amount worth killing for. As a matter of fact, he told them, none of the deaths brought her much financial gain. She went into debt during Buddy's and Marcia's illnesses because she spent so much time with them that her business suffered.

He referred to Mary Beacom as a "so-called" handwriting expert who didn't even attempt to discover who had made the writings she so confidently branded as forgeries. The media's coverage had been "sensational." His client, he said, would never even have been arrested if the police hadn't been trying to appease the outraged citizens of Macon by offering them a scapegoat. He told the jury that Anjette's laughter while Marcia screamed was simply a mother's forced "cheerfulness," designed to ease her child's fears.

"I hope she can live through the heartbreak she must have borne when she walked into a room and had to chuckle to give confidence to an eight-year-old child with hallucinations."

For more than an hour, Buffington fashioned a picture of Anjette Lyles as a caring wife, concerned daughter-in-law and loving mother who had been tragically misunderstood by others. Her fate, he told them, was in their hands.

"You alone will decide whether Anjette Lyles will be cooked by electricity, spend her life in prison or get a medal for being a mother," Buffington reminded them.

The defense rested at 6:30 P.M. and Judge Long recessed for an hour and a half. The jurors walked, in the single file to which they were now accustomed, to a nearby steakhouse for dinner. Meals were ordered as usual and they made the same small talk they had been making for a week, but tonight the end was finally in sight. They were eager to finish a job none of them had enjoyed and get back to their homes and their lives.

In her cell, Anjette was offered dinner, too, but she had little appetite.

"I don't think I can eat anything," she said. She felt limp from the day's effort.

"There's some fresh-baked gingerbread," the matron told her. "What about a piece of that and a glass of sweet milk?"

Anjette smiled. "All right. That'd be nice."

At 8:00 P.M., everyone was back in the courtroom. Judge Long delivered his charge to the jury. As charges in capital cases went, his was rather short. He reviewed what had been presented, and explained that facts concerning the other three deaths for which Anjette had been indicted, but not yet tried, were admissible in this trial based on a Georgia Supreme Court ruling. Circumstantial evidence, he cautioned them, was valid evidence. Finally he laid out the choices before them: guilty, guilty with a recommendation of mercy, and not guilty. He explained that guilty without a recommendation of mercy would result in a sentence of death for the defendant.

At 8:25 P.M., Judge Long dismissed Frank Comer, the one remaining alternate juror, and sent the other twelve men out to deliberate. The first thing the jurors did when they settled in the jury room was to elect Edward Wheeler, a supervisor at nearby Warner Robins Air Force Base, as foreman.

With the judge and jury absent, the mood in the courtroom relaxed. Some of the spectators made their way into the corridor, but most stubbornly stayed where they were, not wanting to chance losing their seats for the final act.

Charles Adams was gathering his papers when Anjette called him to come over where she stood beside the defense table. She gave a big smile to the man whose lunch she had served so often in the past and who had just asked that the jury have her put to death, and told him she didn't hold anything against him.

"Let me hug your neck," she said.

The flustered prosecutor stammered, "You can't do that here, Anjette."

She was still smiling when the deputy led her from the courtroom.

Upstairs Anjette was joined by Byrice Goings. It had already been decided that Byrice would accompany her back to the courtroom when the jury was ready with the verdict, and the jailer's wife was nervous about this new responsibility. While Anjette calmly sipped a Coca-Cola, the other woman paced the cell and worried.

A few minutes before ten, word came that a verdict had been reached and everyone hurried back into the courtroom. The crowd was even larger than it had been earlier, with people standing along the wall at the back of the room.

Byrice anxiously watched the door through which the jury would enter. She had a bottle of ammonia in her purse that she'd snatched up at the last minute, ready for use in case Anjette fainted. The ammonia wasn't the kind sold in tiny bottles for reviving someone in a swoon. It was instead the sudsing variety used for cleaning. There was almost a quart in the large bottle Byrice carried. As they waited for court to resume, Anjette looked over at her friend and happened to glance in the open purse on her lap. What she saw there made her laugh out loud.

"Look at you!" she told Byrice in a low, amused voice. "Your heart's just a-pounding and that ammonia is sloshing away."

Byrice looked down to see the frothy liquid in motion, but before she could say anything in return, a bailiff called "All rise" and Judge Long resumed the bench.

He called the court to order and surveyed the crowded room for a moment. The place was packed with people, and deputies were stationed at every door. Recognizing the potential for chaos, he sternly warned the audience that he would not tolerate any outbursts when the verdict was read, then nodded at the bailiff to bring in the jury.

CHAPTER SEVENTEEN

AT 10:07 P.M., THE JURORS ENTERED THROUGH A SIDE DOOR and took their places on the hard-backed chairs they had occupied for a week. Veteran courtroom watchers examined their faces for some clue as to the verdict they had reached. More than anything else, the jurors just looked tired.

Judge Long asked if they had reached a verdict and Edward Wheeler stood and said they had. A piece of paper was passed to the bailiff who, after showing it to the judge, handed it to Charles Adams to read aloud.

The prosecutor's face was absolutely expressionless as he pronounced the jury's decision: guilty, with no recommendation of mercy.

Jetta and Alice Donovan burst into tears and Byrice Goings' eyes filled, but Anjette's only reaction was to close her eyes briefly. She could feel the heat rise in her face, and observers saw a faint flush of pink wash over her features.

Guilty without recommendation of mercy usually made a death sentence mandatory, but when all of the evidence in a case was circumstantial, the law gave the judge the option of reducing the sentence from death to life imprisonment. However, Oscar Long didn't take the easy way out. Only minutes after the verdict had been announced, he sentenced Anjette Lyles to die in the electric chair at Reidsville State Prison on December fifth.

Anjette kept her face free of emotion and her head high. Jack Gautier immediately made a motion for a new trial. The motion automatically stayed the date of execution.

The judge thanked the jury and they were released. Deputies hurried them out a back door into the chilly night. Most of them were able to avoid the reporters.

Anjette left the courtroom the same way she had entered—stature erect, walk brisk. As she and Byrice crossed the back hallway to the elevator, the crowd that had waited for hours behind the restraining ropes were completely silent. Jetta and Alice were left sobbing in the courtroom. When Lewis Watkins came around the railing and put his arms around his sister, Jetta collapsed against him.

As she left the courtroom, Nora Bagley told a reporter, "She knows how we felt now when we lost Little Ben and my sister and Marcia. Be sure your sins will find you out."

It was quiet in Anjette's cell that night. For once, no prisoners were being booked in below her. After everything that had happened, the silence seemed strange, almost unnatural.

The hearing on the motion for a new trial was set for December 12, but it was unlikely Judge Long would actually hear it that day. The trial had been so lengthy that the transcript was expected to number hundreds of pages and its production was likely to take several months.

The unlikely friendship between Anjette and Byrice continued to grow. From October until January, Anjette was the jail's only female prisoner. When Ollie worked nights, Byrice would have her brought to the apartment where the two women would pass the long fall evenings drinking coffee, chatting and watching television.

On December 2, Anjette was quietly moved from the isolated cell below the courthouse dome back into the women's cell block on the fifth floor. When reporters questioned Sheriff Wood about it, he explained the move was made purely for the convenience of those operating the jail. Anjette certainly didn't object to leaving the room under the dome. Even though there were no other women prisoners at the time, being in the general cell block provided her opportunities to see and speak with some other people.

On December 3, the transcript — 697 pages of testimony and over 500 pages of documentary evidence — was finished and filed in Bibb County Superior Court. Neither the defense nor the prosecution would have time to study the enormous document before December twelfth and Judge Long continued the motion hearing to January twenty-eighth.

Christmas was coming, and although Macon's temperate climate didn't provide the December weather idealized by Currier and Ives, the nights usually brought temperatures down into the thirties and wrapped the town in the appropriate seasonal chill. There were no malls in 1958 and Macon citizens shopped downtown where they always had. Anjette was able to look down from her new cell at the street below and see shoppers loaded with purchases. The bank chimes now played Christmas carols instead of hymns. The sights and sounds filled Anjette with a hollow longing for life as it used to be.

Her pain was eased some by the evenings she spent with Byrice and the children. Debbie was a special delight that year—finally old enough to be excited by the season and the prospect of a visit from Santa. They baked cookies and wrapped presents. Since the Goingses had eight children, there were plenty of presents to wrap.

Byrice pitied this young woman who'd lost one child to death and a second to the courts. She knew Anjette hadn't seen Carla since the day of her arrest. She knew the woman had been convicted of murder—in fact she thought it likely that Anjette had killed her husbands and her mother-in-law—but she did *not* believe she had killed Marcia. It was inconceivable to Byrice that any mother could kill her own child. So she went out of her way to include Anjette in their holiday celebrations.

Anjette spent Christmas Eve in the Goings apartment. After the children were in bed and their mother had checked to be sure they were sleeping, she enlisted Anjette's help.

"Come on," she said, pulling boxes out of a closet, "help me put out Santy Claus."

The two women set the gifts out under the tree, putting together some of the toys and arranging and rearranging the display until it was perfect. Carols played on the radio and the faint scent of evergreen mingled with the cinnamon and vanilla fragrance of the day's baking. It reminded Anjette of other, happier holidays and she had to blink back the tears. She was returned to her cell late that night, but Byrice had her brought back a few hours later in time to see little Debbie Goings's Christmas morning surprise.

1958 slipped into 1959. Anjette passed the time as well as she could, reading or listening to the small radio she was now allowed to keep in her cell. Elvis Presley was a rising star and the Everly Brothers had perfected close harmony, but more and more, she found herself turning the dial to religious broadcasts. Like so many of those imprisoned before her, Anjette now embraced religion with a vengeance. She began writing to local ministers, particularly those who appeared on radio shows, asking them to visit her and pray for her. She even started attending the services held for prisoners in her section of the jail.

In a move that frustrated the media and the curiosity seekers, Judge Long held the hearing on the motion for a new trial in his chambers. At 10:00 A.M. on January 28, the two prosecutors and three defense attorneys met with the judge. The defendant was not present for what was essentially the trading of opinions on points of law. Judge Long patiently heard everyone out, then announced he would take the matter under advisement, and adjourned. The following Monday, he made his decision. To no one's surprise, he refused to grant the motion.

The defense had expected nothing more, of course, but the request for a new trial had to be made and refused before they could move on to the next step. Now that it was behind them, they could begin preparing their appeal to the Supreme Court of Georgia.

In late February, Anjette grew ill with what appeared to be a bad cold, but she was diagnosed with bronchitis and admitted to Macon Hospital. While their client was being treated, Buffington, Gautier and Rhodenhiser worked doggedly to ready the appeal. They scoured the trial transcript for anything that might constitute reversible error. They went over the warrants, the arrest, the commitment hearing and the indictments, searching for any questionable procedures. They finally settled on five points that they believed were grounds for overturning the conviction: the indictment contained no specific date of offense; several witnesses were allowed to testify to facts suggesting that the accused had poisoned three other persons; the prosecution had, by introducing irrelevant material, put Anjette Lyles's character into issue when she had not elected to do so; the jury that tried her was not sworn as required by law; and the evidence, all circumstantial, was not sufficient to convict.

When Anjette was returned to the jail on Saturday, the last day of the month, her attorneys were putting the finishing touches on the appeal. The following Monday, it was filed, and two months later, on May 11, it was heard by the Georgia Supreme Court.

The professional lives of the five Macon attorneys who waited for the Supreme Court to convene in Atlanta that Monday morning had been entangled for over a year by the Lyles murders. Their roles were now ingrained and somewhat confining. They were all more than ready to leave this case and move on to something else, but that was not yet an option.

At 9:00 A.M. the court was called to order. Once again, the defendant's presence was unnecessary. Each side was allotted only a short time to present its case to the seven justices. Gautier and Buffington methodically laid out their list of what they contended were errors in the state's case. Gautier returned to a familiar defense theme: evidence of deaths other than Marcia's should not have been admitted at trial. The admission of such evidence had provided the prosecution an unfair advantage, enabling them to prosecute the one murder which would most appeal to the sympathies of a jury, instead of having to choose the one with the most evidence. Seventy-five percent of the evidence presented at trial, he told them, concerned the deaths of Ben Lyles, Julia Lyles and Buddy Gabbert.

Buffington echoed the popular press when he reminded the justices that if she died in the electric chair, Anjette Lyles would be the first white woman ever executed in Georgia. That statement made a lot of people uneasy in the pre-civil rights South of 1959. However, Buffington said, they weren't looking for sympathy, only justice. The state had presented an inflammatory case to the jury, but had never proved that it was the defendant herself who had administered the poison that killed Marcia Lyles.

When it was time for the state's argument, only Hank O'Neal addressed the court. The Lyles case, he said, was as complete as any poisoning case the Supreme Court had heard and upheld. He cited those cases, one by one, in which evidence of other deaths had been admitted and upheld. After a brief review of the facts of the case, he concluded with an emotional statement of his own.

"This is one of the most atrocious cases this Court has ever been called upon to decide. Marcia Lyles was in the very springtime of her life. Anjette Donovan Lyles should have considered her child a sacred trust. Instead, she murdered her."

The justices typically showed no reaction to the arguments they'd heard. They simply announced that they would take the matter under study, and signaled that the session was over. If past performance were any indication, the decision would not be made public for a month or more. The attorneys were back out in the hot spring sunlight before noon and back in Macon by supper time.

Anjette had always been a naturally optimistic person. While her conviction had been a shock, she'd bounced back in short order. She couldn't help but believe that the case would be overturned and things would turn out her way. As another hot summer settled over the south, she busied herself writing letters, reading, sharing the occasional meal with Byrice and, on nice afternoons, playing on the sun porch with Debbie.

She met with her attorneys late in May to consider the situation. While their client was anticipating good news, the men who had defended her were more worldly. They knew that precious few appeals resulted in overturned convictions and were ready now to consider their options if the appeal were denied. They explained this to Anjette and arranged for her to be examined by two psychiatrists.

The first, Dr. T. E. Shipley, was known for his hypnosis therapy. After a couple of sessions with him, Anjette began behaving strangely. She told the jailers that he'd given her "post-hypnotic suggestions" and caused quite a stir by acting as if she didn't know where she was or what was going on. She found it an amusing way to liven up the long days behind bars.

"She acts like she's forgotten everything," Ollie Goings complained to his wife. "She doesn't know what money is, or people's names, or what a Coca-Cola is. She's giving us some problems here."

Eventually her behavior became disruptive enough that the other inmates began complaining. Ollie decided something had to be done. He had her brought to his office. A lawman for a number of years, he was considerably less inclined to be sympathetic than his soft-hearted wife.

Anjette took a seat in front of his desk. She looked around the room, a puzzled frown creasing her brow. Then she turned her attention to Ollie.

"I ... I don't think I know who you are."

It was too much for the chief jailer. "Anjette, you know good and well who I am. I am sick and tired of you acting like this. You're no more in a post-hypnotic state than I am."

She was momentarily surprised by his outburst. Up until now, everyone had been sympathetic to her. "I'm not hurting anybody," she objected, pouting a little. She resumed the vague expression and gazed into the distance.

But Ollie had a jail to run and other prisoners to think about. His patience was wearing thin. "I guess you didn't hurt anybody when you were killing your child," he snapped.

She reacted as if she'd been slapped and the dreamy, distracted pose vanished with the instinctive need to defend herself. "I didn't do it!"

Goings didn't argue the point. He just sent her back to her cell. Post-hypnotic suggestions were never mentioned again.

But the psychiatrists weren't through with Anjette nor she with them. A second doctor—this time a woman—followed the first. She spent a whole day interviewing Anjette in the jail's conference room and Byrice Goings was tapped to sit in on the sessions. Anjette understood that behaving well would earn her nothing. From what she'd gathered from her attorneys, being considered insane was to her advantage. So she amused herself by being deliberately difficult, acting as if she didn't understand what was going on and fashioning answers that made no sense. Byrice had never seen her behave that way.

When they interrupted the session for lunch, the other women in Anjette's cell block had already eaten, so Byrice took her back to her apartment where the maid prepared a meal for the two of them. As they began eating, she asked Anjette how she was holding up.

"I'm fine," Anjette said with a laugh, "but that psychiatrist has just about had it with me. By this afternoon when I get through with her, she'll be crazy as hell!"

Anjette was true to her word. She continued to act out for the rest of the afternoon. It was a very long day for the doctor.

Odd though it seemed under the circumstances, Anjette was a romantic. The only times she could remember being happy, *really* happy, were those times when she was falling in love. She adored the excitement, the thrill of the beginnings of love. It was only after the relationship became routine that she grew bored and began seeing the other person's faults.

She hadn't experienced that kind of excitement in more than a year. After she was moved back to the general population of the jail, she began taking notice of some of the male inmates. One young man in particular caught her eye. He was handsome, even in the prison uniform, and when he smiled, he had a wicked gleam in his eye. She started looking forward to catching a glimpse of him. Once or twice, the two even exchanged a few words. She didn't know if he even noticed her, but that didn't seem to matter much. It might have seemed childish to someone on the outside, but the minor flirtation became an important part of Anjette's days.

On July 8, the Supreme Court ruled. In a six to one decision, the conviction and sentence were upheld. The majority opinion, written by Justice Tom Candler, dismissed the defense's grounds for appeal and was uncompromising in its portrayal of Anjette Lyles as a cold-blooded murderer.

"The evidence as we view it after careful examination shows nothing short of a deliberate, premeditated, well-concocted plan and scheme to murder an innocent child for no cause except to satisfy her selfish desire for money."

No advance notice of the decision had been given, so no one was able to warn Anjette. She was in her cell listening to the radio when she heard a news bulletin that her appeal had been denied. For once, the icy calm broke. Mrs. Joe Stripling, the matron, heard Anjette screaming her name and came running. When she entered the cell, the prisoner burst into tears. The older woman did her best to comfort her, but Anjette sobbed uncontrollably. She had honestly expected the verdict to be overturned. Now for the first time since her arrest, she was forced to confront the real possibility she would be executed.

The jail administration relaxed their rules that afternoon and allowed Anjette to have visitors. Her mother came, as did Alice Donovan and Lewis Watkins. About 5:00 P.M., Agnes Claire Arnold, a local evangelist, arrived. She stayed over an hour with Anjette, praying and speaking in quiet tones. By evening, the prisoner had regained much of her control, but she was still nervous and jumpy. She ate only a small supper, chain smoked cigarettes and drank Coca-Colas.

Her attorneys filed for a rehearing by the Supreme Court, but the action made little impression on Anjette. She couldn't believe the appeal had failed. Her disappointment became depression. She was listless, dragging around, rarely speaking. She suffered fainting spells. Although she still met with the ministers, she was inattentive to their words and hardly ever offered any of her own. Byrice tried to cheer her up, tempt her with little treats, but she couldn't penetrate the wall of despair.

The Supreme Court took much less time to consider the request for a rehearing than it had the original appeal. A week after it was filed, the request was denied without comment. Roy Rhodenhiser rushed to the courthouse as soon as he heard. Agnes Claire Arnold was again visiting with Anjette. He told the jailers that he had to see his client immediately. Anjette was brought to the conference room, leaving the evangelist waiting in the hallway.

"What is it?" she asked fearfully.

As gently as he could, Rhodenhiser explained that their request had been denied. Anjette nodded. She didn't speak. She walked into the corridor and promptly fainted, pitching forward on her face. Arnold rushed forward to help revive her and the matron brought a cloth to wipe her face. She didn't say a word as they led her back to her cell.

The next move was Judge Long's. With the appeal denied, the execution date had to be reset. The hearing was arranged, with little fanfare, for July 28.

Anjette had a few bad minutes in her cell that Tuesday morning. She didn't want to go back into that courtroom. She had a panicky impulse to run and hide. But then reason and her own strong will came to her rescue. She put on a subdued sleeveless dark blue dress, patterned with yellow, and pulled her white hair back into a ponytail. When she entered the courtroom just before nine, Byrice was by her side. The two women joined the attorneys at the defense table. Once again, Byrice was the more nervous of the two.

As soon as Judge Long called the session to order, Roy Rhodenhiser was on his feet with a motion. He reminded the judge that it was within his discretion to sentence Anjette to life rather than death and asked that it be done.

Judge Long's reply was terse. "The Court will have to deny that motion."

He then went immediately to the business at hand and sentenced Anjette Lyles to be executed between 10:00 A.M. and 2:00 P.M. on August 17. As usual, she showed no outward reaction. When court adjourned, she rose quickly to her feet. Her steps were quick and sure as she left the courtroom with Byrice hurrying behind her. She didn't seem to notice the camera flashes or the questions shouted at her by the crowd of reporters.

While the local papers reported the resentencing, with the knee-jerk reference to the fact that Lyles would be the first white woman ever executed in Georgia, Sheriff Wood began arrangements to move the prisoner. With the execution date set, the law required that she be taken to the place of execution to wait for the sentence to be carried out. In Georgia, the place of execution was Reidsville State Prison, located some hundred miles to the southeast in a sparsely populated section of the coastal plain. Anjette was to be taken to Reidsville on August 4, less than two weeks before she was scheduled to die.

CHAPTER EIGHTEEN

HER ATTORNEYS GRIMLY MOVED ON TO THE NEXT STEP IN THE process of trying to save Anjette's life. The Board of Pardons and Paroles could commute a death sentence, but they could not hear an appeal for commutation while an execution date was in force. The only way the execution could be forestalled and the case reviewed by the Board was through a gubernatorial stay. By the afternoon of the day she was resentenced, the defense team had already begun forming the plea to Governor Ernest Vandiver.

The night before she was scheduled to leave Macon, reporters were caught by surprise when Anjette, through her attorneys, agreed to meet with them. In the jail's conference room, she gave her first interview since her arrest.

Anjette concentrated on being pleasant and agreeable. The reporters found her attitude reminiscent of the days when she was the most popular restaurateur in town. The first questions predictably were how she felt about the impending execution.

"I want to live as good as the next one," she told them, "to raise the other little girl I've got, because I was a good mother. I stayed at home at night and didn't run around."

"Anjette, are you afraid of dying?"

"Everyone's afraid to die. I don't want to die, but I feel in my heart I'm ready to die if I have to."

She readily acknowledged she had done wrong—but only in regards to the forging of Julia Lyles's will. "I'm ashamed of it and I'm sorry for it. What I did wrong wouldn't have amounted to much of anything. I don't know how it would have turned out."

Several times they asked her bluntly if she were guilty of any of the murders. The answer was always the same. "I didn't murder. I didn't kill. I couldn't have stood it up here for fifteen months if I had killed all those people."

As the interview progressed, Anjette dropped dark hints about who might really be responsible for the four deaths. She knew that her attorneys wouldn't want her to talk too much—they never did—but she couldn't resist a few words.

"I know a lot I'd like to say," she told them, "but I don't think this is the time to say it. I might lose my life, but the person that did these things will suffer a lot more. People don't know the truth about it. There's a lot more to it than they know. People can live a lie just so long. They'll catch up with them. You know, when I'm gone, you can't bring me back."

Word of her new interest in religion had gotten out and she was asked about it.

"I could do a lot of good work, even in prison." A serene smile curved her lips. "Even in this jail I've gotten on my knees with girls and prayed with them and I've talked to them and read the Bible to them. I've got enough religion in me. I've found God enough to know if I were to die, I would not die with a lie on my lips, because that's the one person you cannot lie to is God. He knows and I know."

The thing she wanted most, of course, was freedom, and she assured them that if she were released she would be a changed woman.

"I would stay out of nightclubs and go to church, live more for God because God is the only one who can really help. This has brought me to God, this really has."

At 9:00 on Tuesday morning, she was ready for the trip to Reidsville. She hugged Byrice and told her goodbye. As she and the deputies made their way through the first floor lobby, several people shouted goodbye to her.

"Bye," she called. "Pray for me."

Sheriff Wood himself drove the county car to Reidsville and Ollie Goings sat in the front passenger seat. Latrelle West was once again pressed into duty and shared the back seat with Anjette and Deputy Walter Walron. Anjette wore the same dark blue dress she'd worn when she was sentenced to death for the second time. Both she and West wore dark glasses as protection against the glaring August sun.

Anjette's optimism had resurfaced. She refused to believe that she would be executed. Because she made such a determined effort to keep things upbeat, it was a surprisingly light-hearted trip. She and West laughed together like old friends. When Wood took a wrong turn, his passengers teased him about getting lost and not being able to find the prison.

As they neared Reidsville, the cheerful mood slipped a bit. The occupants of the car had to face the unsettling truth that they weren't just out for a leisurely ride in the country. The five of them were, instead, en route to a dismal maximum security prison where in less than two weeks, one of them would be strapped into a wooden chair and electrocuted.

They stopped at a guardhouse where Sheriff Wood had a brief conversation with the man at the gate. Then they were waved through and Wood parked the car. They walked across the yard and into the prison. Anjette carried a Bible, a pack of cigarettes and a wallet. Sheriff Wood followed with a small bag that held two pair of pajamas and a few toiletries.

Warden R. P. Balkom met them in the lobby. A kind, introspective forty-four year old Macon native who'd worked at Reidsville since 1939, he had begun his career at the prison as business manager. He had taken the job of warden only on condition that he not ever be required to observe an execution. For Balkom, Anjette was a major problem.

She was taken immediately to the prison hospital where she was examined and x-rayed. She removed her street clothes—she was allowed to keep her watch and a ring—and donned pajamas, prison-issued slippers and a robe. These were the only clothes she would be allowed to wear while at Reidsville. Next she was photographed and given a UDS (Under Death Sentence) number. Finally, prodded and processed and appropriately dressed, she was led, by a circuitous route that kept her from contact with any other prisoner, to the fifth floor in the building referred to as the "death house." There she was locked in a steel-barred cell only eighty feet away from the room containing the electric chair.

Reidsville was the state's largest prison and housed almost twenty-five hundred inmates, but only one hundred and eighty of them were women and, before Anjette's arrival, none of those women were condemned to death. That August there was only one prisoner—a man—awaiting execution. Anjette's arrival made it necessary to move him to another building. And this was not the only special arrangement made to accommodate her. In its history, only one woman had been executed there—Lena Baker in 1945 and she had been, as the newspapers were so fond of reminding everyone, a black woman. Faced with Anjette Lyles, the prison administration didn't quite know what to do.

Two matrons were hired at a cost of $30 a day as special guards for her. One of the two would be stationed outside her cell twenty-four hours a day. The only time Anjette would leave her cell would be for a daily shower in a room a few steps down the corridor. The only other people she would see were those trustees who brought her meals.

Anjette wasn't distressed by her circumstances. She had convinced herself she wouldn't be executed. When Ollie Goings came to say goodbye, he found her in good spirits.

"You'll be back next week," she told him confidently. "They aren't going to keep me here."

Anjette's attorneys formally requested that the governor grant her a 90-day stay of execution to provide them with time to present the Board of Pardons and Paroles their motion to have Anjette's sentence commuted to life. They announced this at a press conference. There had been, they said, considerable deterioration in their client's mental state since her conviction. While she had given the appearance of understanding right from wrong at her trial, exhaustive tests had proven she was suffering from "psychosis—a schizophrenic reaction, mixed type, with paranoid and hebephrenic features".

The next day the special prosecutors fired off their own letter to Vandiver, advising him that they opposed the granting of a 90-day stay, calling it an unreasonable length of time. They did concede that if the Board thought it necessary, they would not object to a shorter stay of execution. But they cautioned they would never agree to a commutation of Lyles's sentence.

"We believe," the letter continued, "every one of her victims would have wanted a 90-day extension to live, but Mrs. Lyles served as judge, jury and executioner."

After receiving notice from the defense, the Board of Pardons and Paroles made its own plea to the governor, asking that he grant a stay in the case to allow "more time for a thorough consideration of the case."

While this legal and political maneuvering took place in Macon and Atlanta, Anjette settled into the institutional routine at Reidsville. She chatted with the matrons and got to know some of the trustees. When the other female inmates learned that Anjette was being held in the death house, they made her a pair of shorty pajamas as a gesture of friendship. She was delighted with the homey gift. The pajamas she had brought with her had sleeves and trouser-style legs. The new abbreviated garments would be much more comfortable during the hot August days.

On August 10, Governor Vandiver met with the defense attorneys for only ten minutes or so before signing an executive order granting Anjette Lyles a 60-day stay of execution. The Board of Pardons and Paroles immediately set down a hearing date of September 22.

At Reidsville Prison, Anjette heard the news from a small radio in her cell just moments before Assistant Warden Lamont Smith showed up there to advise her officially that her execution had been delayed.

"You just don't know the feeling inside me!" she told him joyously. But she wasn't surprised. She had known that her life wasn't going to end in the electric chair.

Once again, the Lyles case was news in Macon. Anjette's stay of execution knocked the two big stories of the day—the impending visit to the United States by Nikita Khrushchev and a record-breaking heat wave—off the front page. The reprieve also caused an immediate conflict between state authorities and those in Bibb county.

The Board of Corrections wanted Anjette returned immediately to the Bibb County Jail. While they would never acknowledge it publicly, the staff at Reidsville were anxious to see the last of Anjette Lyles. Her presence at the prison had been unsettling for everyone. In addition to attracting the attention of the whole state and drawing reporters like flies to honey, Anjette's time there created unexpected problems with the male trustees who delivered her meals and cleaned up that section of the building. Her effect on them was no different than it had been on the other men she'd encountered in her life. Even in prison awaiting execution, she exercised her legendary charm. The men competed with each other to be allowed to deliver her food, and would slip in after hours to see her and bring her gifts.

The Macon authorities thought she should remain at Reidsville until the Board made its decision. They felt she was under an order of execution and should stay at the place of execution.

The governor himself finally broke the deadlock. On August 13, he issued another executive order directing that she be returned to the

Bibb County Jail. The next day, Chief Deputy Billy Murphy, Investigators Harry Harris and Joe Brown, and Latrelle West made the drive back to Reidsville.

Anjette was less animated during the trip back to Macon than when she had been taken to the prison eleven days before, although she did laugh when she talked about the weight she had gained while at Reidsville, blaming it on the good food there. She wore the same dress in which she had arrived, but told her companions that she had almost been unable to zip it up. In addition to the meals, she confided that the trustees had brought her Coca-Colas and ice cream at night.

Returning to the Bibb County Jail was almost like a homecoming. Everywhere she looked there were familiar sights and faces. Several people in the corridors greeted her and wished her good luck. She was put back in the women's cell block and Byrice Goings was there to welcome her. She fell back into her old routine.

On a hot afternoon about a week later, Byrice had Anjette brought to her apartment.

"Come out on the sun porch with me," she said. "There's someone I want you to see."

She led Anjette to the terrace wall and pointed to the park five stories below. There, for the first time in over a year, she saw Carla. It was hard to get a good look at her from this distance, but the child's movements were so familiar that there couldn't be any doubt it was she. Anjette couldn't hold back her tears.

"Why would they think I could do that to Marcia?" she asked when she could speak again. "What is Carla going to think?"

After a short while, Carla was led away, never aware that her mother had been watching her from above. Anjette sobbed in Byrice's arms while the other woman murmured useless words of comfort. As the storm of tears subsided, Anjette took a deep, shuddering breath, blew her nose and wiped her eyes.

"It's all right," she said finally. "Carla knows that I love her and I loved Marcia."

In September, Anjette gave another interview to the press. On a Saturday afternoon, she met with George Doss of the *Macon Telegraph* and Howard Absalom of WMAZ in the jail conference room. William Buffington, Sheriff Wood and Ollie Goings sat in on the forty-five-minute interview. Several people, including Anjette, were smoking and the haze grew thick and irritating in the small room. Wearing the sleeveless blue dress that had become her public uniform, she sat on one side of the table with the reporters opposite. The other men were as inconspicuous as possible, chairs shoved back against the wall.

Anjette spoke calmly of the upcoming hearing before the Board of Pardons and Paroles. She was praying, she said, for them to commute her sentence.

When one of the reporters asked about a remark she had made while at Reidsville that there was one particular person she wanted to see in Macon, she smiled mysteriously and confessed that there was, indeed, a special man she longed to see, but she refused to name him.

"I've been in love with him for a long time" was all she would tell them. "I knew him before all this came up. If ever I do go to death row again, I'm certainly going to ask to see him."

Talk then turned to Carla. Anjette declared she missed the child desperately, but wouldn't ask to have her visit the jail.

"I'm praying so hard for a life sentence, more for my little girl than for myself. If I get the electric chair, she'll never live it down. She's just eight years old. I'm more concerned about her than I am for myself. I did love my children—I was a good mother. I just can't see how I got where I am today."

She acknowledged that she had been seeing some psychiatrists on a more or less constant basis, but they hadn't discussed diagnoses with her. "They let you do all the talking and they just listen."

The Pardons and Paroles hearing was scheduled for September 22, the day before Anjette's thirty-fourth birthday. While Khrushchev toured the Midwest, annoying Americans with remarks about Soviet farming superiority, the Georgia Pardons and Paroles Board convened on the third floor of the Capitol Building in Atlanta. The defendant was not present, but her mother and sister-in-law sat at the defense table with her three attorneys. The prosecutors sat only a few feet away.

Buffington explained that their grounds for appeal were simple— Anjette Lyles was insane. The first defense witness, who would spend most of the day testifying, was presented to prove just that. Dark-browed and bespectacled, Tragan E. Shipley was an Atlanta psychiatrist who had examined Anjette several times. He had, he told them, found her to be an excellent subject for hypnosis. Under hypnosis, he had regressed her to the day after her birth when she had displayed reflexes possible only for a newborn, thus proving she was in fact in a deep trance state. This testimony came at a time when Americans had become fascinated with the Bridey Murphy case and Shipley's testimony was sure to receive national coverage.

He testified he had, while she was in a trance, led her into the future and had her experience her own death in the electric chair and her ascent afterwards to heaven. Through it all, she had maintained her innocence.

Then Shipley dropped a bombshell. "Mrs. Lyles told me, both in ordinary conversation and under hypnosis, that it was her mother, Jetta Donovan, who had poisoned Marcia."

Jetta stared at him for a long minute, then began to cry.

Anjette had also declared, the doctor said, that Julia Lyles had been responsible for the deaths of Ben Lyles, Buddy Gabbert and herself. To demonstrate that Anjette truly believed these statements, Shipley testified that he'd given her a post-hypnotic suggestion that lying would cause her to have severe headaches. When she had made these same statements after he'd brought her out of her trance, he said she had shown no indication that she experienced pain of any kind.

At one point, Board Chairman Hugh Carney interrupted the testimony to ask the psychiatrist if he couldn't corroborate Anjette's statements by placing Jetta Donovan under hypnosis. The suggestion brought forth a near-hysterical wail from the woman. She began sobbing and collapsed on the defense table, her head on her arms. The hearing was recessed and Alice Donovan led Jetta from the room.

When testimony resumed, Dr. Shipley informed the Board that he was not inclined to try and hypnotize Jetta. Even if she would consent, and that was doubtful in itself, he didn't believe it would be of any help.

"I have seen few people who can talk faster than she can. I don't mean to be disrespectful, but such people are not easily hypnotized to the state where Anjette was."

His diagnosis was definite. Anjette Lyles was schizophrenic with symptoms of paranoia. He said she experienced hallucinations, including seeing angels flying around the room and trying to catch them. He related that she had once told him she caught some and put them in a jar for him to see, but they had gotten away. She was, he said, "in layman's terms, insane."

He was less positive as to her guilt or innocence. "Frankly, I don't know. I've tried many ways to shake her story, and I don't know."

By late afternoon, Jetta Donovan was calm enough to return to the hearing and make an unsworn statement. She first assured them that she had not killed her granddaughter, then tearfully begged the Board to show mercy to her daughter. Anjette's problems were mental in origin, she said, and she begged them to spare her life.

The Board adjourned for the day.

The hearing had returned Jetta Donovan to the spotlight—a position she despised. When the afternoon session ended, she was hounded by the news media. She and Alice had managed to elude most of them, but as they were leaving the building, Jetta spotted a photographer looming like a vulture in the stairwell above them. She grabbed Alice as a shield and pulled her back into the hallway. They retreated as fast as they could, eventually emerging from a back door into the hot afternoon, unphotographed.

Anjette passed her thirty-fourth birthday quietly in her cell. She was pleasantly surprised to receive birthday cards from all over the country.

"They're from people I don't even know," she told Byrice. "And some of them had money in them. Can you believe that?"

In Atlanta, the hearing to determine her fate continued. The defense called a second psychiatrist, Winston Burdine, who agreed with Dr. Shipley's diagnosis that Anjette Lyles was schizophrenic.

"I thought she was insane each time I examined her," he said. "At first I thought she knew right from wrong, but later I had my doubts. I think Anjette Lyles will continue to get worse the rest of her life. She'll deteriorate mentally at a rapid rate. Her mental condition will become progressively worse."

When asked when he first realized how serious Anjette's mental condition had become, Burdine was definite. "I realized she was growing worse when she began to gain weight and to twitch."

Facial twitches, he advised, were often signs of insanity.

Burdine was followed by psychologist Myron T. Weiner, who had administered a battery of tests to Anjette. He agreed with the two psychiatrists that the woman was insane.

"In 1958, she made sense in conversation, but this is no longer true. It is almost impossible for her to carry on a normal conversation now. She is definitely insane."

When they presented their rebuttal, the prosecution introduced a love letter written by Anjette to a man named Eddie Boyle. It became apparent that this must be the man to whom she had referred during her interview with the Macon press. The letter came into the prosecution's possession in an unusual manner. Charles Edward Boyle, Charles Adams explained, was a Macon cab driver with a petty criminal record. He had been serving time at the Macon stockade on a public drunk charge when Anjette wrote to him at that address. However, by the time the letter arrived, he had escaped. The letter was returned to the Bibb County Jail as undeliverable and came to the attention of the jail authorities. Boyle was now back in the stockade, serving out the remainder of his sentence, as well as some extra time for escape.

Adams showed the letter to the members of the Board. "This letter is not the random rambling of an insane person," he said. "It is rational and coherent."

Adams was highly critical of the defense and their psychiatrist for even raising the possibility that Jetta Donovan had killed Marcia Lyles.

"Dr. Shipley perpetrated or aided in the perpetration of the cruelest hoax I've ever witnessed. There was no reason to embarrass Mrs. Donovan that way." He described how she had stood by Anjette throughout the trial and continued to stand by her even now. "Anjette wasn't nearly as good a mother as Jetta Donovan has been."

CHAPTER NINETEEN

WHILE THOSE INVOLVED WAITED IMPATIENTLY, THE PARDONS and Paroles Board deliberated over Anjette's case. They were faced with two equally unpleasant options. If they found that the defendant was insane and commuted her sentence, they risked public outrage. There was strong sentiment in the state that she should be punished for the shocking murder of her daughter. On the other hand, failure to commute the sentence would send a white woman to the electric chair for the first time in the state's history. After days of debate and discussion, they hit upon a way to avoid both unappealing altern- atives—they would make no decision. Instead they requested that Governor Vandiver appoint a Sanity Commission to determine whether Anjette was insane. The governor complied with the request and appointed three medical professionals—two psychiatrists and a medical doctor—to serve on the commission and report their findings to him.

The three doctors—William Rottersman, Bernard Holland and R. W. Bradford—met at the Bibb County Jail on a sunny October afternoon where they spent several hours examining Anjette Lyles in the conference room. The following day, a psychologist from Dr. Holland's Emory Hospital staff, spent an additional two hours administering tests to the condemned woman. Anjette's behavior with these doctors was as erratic and bizarre as it had been with the earlier psychiatrists. But she didn't joke about it this time.

When the commission met Wednesday night in Atlanta to compare notes, they were unanimous in their decision. Anjette Lyles was insane. Their report was forwarded to Governor Vandiver the next day. It read in part:

"The type of her mental illness is chronic paranoid schizophrenic. It is our opinion that Mrs. Anjette Donovan Lyles, from her earliest years, has felt unloved and unwanted by her parents. During her formative and school years, Mrs. Lyles felt unaccepted by her schoolmates. In later years, despite her apparent social adjustment, she was unable to feel close to and accepted by other people."

She had been hostile and suspicious during their examination, the report stated, and it was difficult to pinpoint the exact time at which she became obviously psychotic. Their prediction was that her condition would only deteriorate.

Her attorneys met with her after the commission's decision had been sent to the Governor.

"Georgia law expressly forbids the execution of an insane person," Buffington told her. "So you will not be put to death."

She thanked them profusely. She had known everything would be all right and now it was.

But, they explained, the decision didn't mean freedom for her. She would be held in the state hospital for the insane at Milledgeville until such time as she recovered enough to have her sentence carried out.

It took a moment for the reality of the situation to penetrate. "You mean I'll have to stay there always?"

"Unless the doctors think you have recovered—that you're sane again. And then you'll be taken to Reidsville and executed."

Buffington, Rhodenhiser and Gautier issued a joint statement thanking the governor and the commission. Justice, they declared, had been served.

The two special prosecutors reacted angrily to the commission's report.

"It appears that psychiatry and psychologists are taking over the work of the courts," Charles Adams told reporters furiously. "The Governor should have the Sanity Commission examined to determine as to whether or not knowing the difference between right and wrong is still the meaning of legal insanity. And Anjette Lyles is entitled to receive the Academy Award as the best actress of 1959."

Anjette met with Ollie Goings a little later and persuaded him to telephone Atlanta reporter Celestine Sibley for her. She wanted Sibley to have the first interview with her now that it was sure she wouldn't be executed. Sibley and a photographer drove to Macon the same day and met with Anjette at the jail.

"I'm happy God has spared my life," Anjette told her. But she was unhappy with the idea that people would believe she was insane. "I don't think I'm crazy. But at least my child can live this down. She couldn't live it down if I went to the electric chair."

Sibley told her of Adams's remarks about the Academy Award.

"I didn't act. I haven't acted any part of it. I just sat right there in the chair and talked to those doctors like I'd talk to anybody else. I answered their questions as best I could."

As the interview was winding down, Sibley asked, "Anjette, you've worked all your life. What are you going to do in Milledgeville?"

Anjette just shrugged. "I don't have any idea. I don't know what they have to do there."

"Well, I think there's a sewing room at the hospital. That might help pass the time away."

Anjette laughed aloud. "Celestine, I couldn't sew a stitch to save my life. All I know is food."

Charles Adams and Hank O'Neal sent a letter to Attorney General Eugene Cook resigning their positions as special prosecutors and made a copy of it available to the press.

"Since this case was terminated in the courts, it has been controlled by the governor and the parole board. We cannot agree in any way with the methods they have employed. The Supreme Court of the United States was taken over by the psychologists several years ago, but we are quite surprised to see it happen in Georgia.

"We are unwilling to assume responsibilities for the results of actions in which local authorities have no voice whatsoever. Our only hope is that the staff in Milledgeville can protect the other inmates from the horrible death suffered by her daughter, two husbands and mother-in-law."

Around noon on Saturday, October 17, Anjette Lyles left the Bibb County Jail for the last time, accompanied by Ollie and Byrice Goings. They got into a sheriff's department car driven by Captain Bill Adams for the thirty mile ride to Milledgeville. It was a gray autumn day, windy with a threat of rain, and Anjette's brightly patterned yellow dress did little to lighten the mood.

Milledgeville is a small town of wide streets and graceful old white houses, a town that had served for a while as Georgia's capital. But once the state hospital for the insane was located there, Milledgeville became synonymous with madness. In 1959, being sent to Milledgeville meant only one thing and it had nothing to do with antebellum homes.

Anjette was more frightened of this destination that she had been of Reidsville. The hospital had a terrifying reputation as a place of neglect and mistreatment. She reached out and held Byrice's hand as the car turned in the drive and the big, ugly buildings came into view.

In the lobby, she said goodbye to Ollie and Byrice.

"Don't you worry now," Byrice told her, giving her a hug. "I'll come and visit you. And I'll bring Debbie, too."

Anjette nodded, holding back the tears that threatened. "Take care of yourself. I'll see you soon."

Just like at Reidsville, Anjette's street clothes were taken from her. She was made to take a shower, and was issued a shapeless cotton dress and slippers. They took her to a room in the Powell Building, a huge, glaringly white structure that was used for the administration of the hospital as well as for housing some of the inmates. Over the next few weeks, she would be given a battery of tests, both physical and mental, in order for the hospital personnel to evaluate her. She would then be placed in one of the women's wards and treated like any other inmate. While male patients who had been convicted of murder and sent to the state hospital were locked away in a secure building, no such facility was available for women. And the staff didn't anticipate needing such a thing for Anjette. She might have caused the slow, agonizing deaths of four people, but she had never been physically violent.

After her initial testing was complete, Anjette was permanently assigned to quarters on the third floor of the Powell Building with seventy other women. She settled into the dull hospital routine. She was a compliant patient, doing whatever she was told and never complaining. Like the other inmates, she was allowed guests every day but Sunday, and she had her share. Family members came to see her regularly, and Byrice Goings visited at least once a month.

Anjette devoted more and more time to mysticism. She read any books she could find on the subject and could talk about magic and voodoo and her belief in it for hours on end. She was not allowed candles, but often used playing cards to predict the future.

"There's not much change in her condition," hospital director Dr. Irville H. McKinnon told reporters on the six month anniversary of her arrival. "She is now in practically the same condition she was in when she came to the hospital."

While she may not have been legally competent, there is no doubt that Anjette understood the significance of the periodic testing to which she was subjected, and the importance of maintaining the insanity diagnosis.

"What have you been doing, honey?" Byrice asked during one of her visits.

"They did another evaluation on me yesterday."

"Oh. Have you heard any results?"

Anjette laughed. "They think I'm crazy as hell and I'm going to let them keep thinking it. Because if they don't, they're going to fry my ass!"

Anjette continued to gain weight, and grew very self-conscious about it. She told the staff members she didn't want outsiders to see her.

"I've had enough of people pointing at me and watching me," she said.

As the months and years passed, she became more and more withdrawn. She spent most of her time alone, rarely interacting with the other women. She was now a fat woman in a baggy gray dress living in a gray world. But she didn't forget Byrice. Every Mother's Day, she sent her a card signed with love. Byrice continued her visits. She sometimes brought Debbie to visit her "Jette," and Anjette had the pleasure of watching the child grow up. Sometimes Byrice would bring her special food—chocolate cake was her favorite.

Anjette Lyles, the notorious murderer many people believed to be the most evil woman ever produced by the state of Georgia, died quietly of heart failure at the Milledgeville State Hospital on December 4, 1977. She was fifty-two years old. She was buried in the churchyard at Coleman's Chapel in Wadley beside Ben and Marcia Lyles.

INDEX